PALLIATIVE CARE, AGEING AND SPIRITUALITY

A Guide for Older People, Carers and Families

ELIZABETH MACKINLAY

Jessica Kingsley *Publishers*
London and Philadelphia

First published in 2012
by Jessica Kingsley Publishers
116 Pentonville Road
London N1 9JB, UK
and
400 Market Street, Suite 400
Philadelphia, PA 19106, USA

www.jkp.com

Library of Congress Cataloging in Publication Data
MacKinlay, Elizabeth, 1940-
Palliative care, ageing, and spirituality : a guide for older people, carers, and families / Elizabeth MacKinlay.
p. cm.
Includes bibliographical references and index.
ISBN 978-1-84905-290-0 (alk. paper)
1. Terminal care. 2. Palliative treatment. 3. Caregivers. 4. Death. 5. Spirituality. I. Title. II. Title: Palliative care, ageing, and spirituality.
R726.8.M24 2012
616.029--dc23
2011034747

British Library Cataloguing in Publication Data
A CIP catalogue record for this book is available from the British Library

ISBN 978 1 84905 290 0
eISBN 978 0 85700 598 4

Printed and bound in Great Britain

This book is dedicated to the memory of
Gabrielle Brian and Lewis Elliott

ACKNOWLEDGEMENTS

This book would not have been written without the able support of the team comprised of Anne Hand, Judith Marston and Dorothy Seidel-Hooke. Together we explored the possibilities and need for the book, undertook research to collect the material together and arrange it.

We acknowledge the valuable contribution of a grant from the Australian Capital Territory (ACT) Palliative Care Society that helped fund the research for the book.

Wendy Elliott, as a care partner, kept a journal during the last part of her husband Lewis' life. Her permission to draw on this journal is greatly appreciated.

Gabrielle Brian wrote a reflective journal from the time that she had surgery for brain tumours until she could no longer write or speak. Her work is reproduced with permission and is greatly appreciated.

John's stories of his experiences with his wife who was dying are used with permission and are very much appreciated.

CONTENTS

PALLIATIVE CARE, AGEING AND SPIRITUALITY

by the same author

Ageing and Spirituality across Faiths and Cultures
Edited by Elizabeth MacKinlay
ISBN 978 1 84905 006 7

Ageing, Disability and Spirituality
Addressing the Challenge of Disability in Later Life
Edited by Elizabeth MacKinlay
ISBN 978 1 84310 584 8

Spiritual Growth and Care in the Fourth Age of Life
Elizabeth MacKinlay
ISBN 978 1 84310 231 1

The Spiritual Dimension of Ageing
Elizabeth MacKinlay
ISBN 978 1 84310 008 9

PREFACE

This book is written as a guide for those older people who are dying and their loved ones as they make this important final journey of life. However, it may also be of value to those who provide care for older people in community or residential care. The book may serve as a resource for holistic care. Dying is so often feared in current western societies; largely it is a fear of the unknown, but it is also a fear built on the basis of a society that sees death as failure. This book seeks to uncover the process of this final life career into death as a part of life through which there is still hope and a time in which loved ones can grow, strengthened by the hard times that they face together. For those who have a religious faith, this is a time of moving closer to God and, for Christians, the promise of eternal life. For the many without a religious faith, being able to face this final life career with loved ones, being able to speak of death at emotional and spiritual levels, can be a source of strength for all – those who care and those who are dying. The focus of this book is on the often unspoken things; the emotional and spiritual aspects of dying and death, acknowledging that death does lie ahead (as it does for each one of us). In contrast, I have focused little on the physical aspects of dying, except where I believe a fuller account may be helpful to the reader – for instance, in the final stages of dying. Obviously, pain is an important topic, so I have included accounts of both physical and existential (related to meaning, suffering and deep yearning) pain. I have addressed common myths about pain and enlarged on effective pain management.

In this small book I have attempted to avoid the use of jargon and to engage with readers in ways that will support them in the journey that lies ahead.

INTRODUCTION

ABOUT GROWING OLDER, DYING AND DEATH

In this short book, we are talking about dying and about death. This is the last important journey that each of us takes in life. This journey is an important one, one that we each want to get 'right'. But how do we do that when we don't have a clear pattern to tell us how best to travel this final life journey? Michael Barbato (2005) and others have emphasised the purpose of this journey as a time to reflect on life and to prepare for death. These days, that purpose is often clouded and confused by the vast array of technology that can support the dying process long after it has become futile to treat the person with any hope of success. The experience of each dying person and his or her family is unique, but there are also similarities of experience with others.

The variety of experiences is found first in the physical symptoms of disease and the way that these play out in the dying process. As well, the person brings his or her whole life experience into this process of dying; his or her genetic background, ways of coping, beliefs and culture, educational background and family supports. Yet another influence on the quality of the dying experience is the myths that the person and their family may hold. All of these will influence the way the person sees the dying process and how he or she will be able to face it. Hope and fear are important components of this, as are attitudes to life and to death.

The purpose of this book is to provide a guide to living in the face of dying. It is a book written especially for older[1] people who are facing death, through different kinds of experiences, perhaps through frailty of later life, perhaps through chronic illnesses, including stroke, cancer and other diseases, perhaps through dementia. It is also a book for those who walk this journey with people who are dying: their loved ones and those who provide care. This book focuses on a holistic view of the process of dying. It addresses questions such as 'What does it feel like to be facing my own death? What does it feel like to journey with my loved one in the final stages of life?'

Some aspects of physical dying will be addressed, but the focus of this book is on psychosocial, emotional and spiritual issues of the 'final life career'. The term 'final life career' is used deliberately to indicate that this last stage is still an important part of life. Too often in the twentieth century in western societies death was hidden from view and taken out of control of those who were dying and their families. The final life career is a time of preparing for this final journey and it is also a time of handing over to the coming generations. It can be a time of struggle, but also of joy and completion; a journey that, at best, is travelled together with loved ones and carers.

Part of the focus in this handbook is on the experiences of others, who are either living the experience of dying themselves, or are primary carers for someone who is

---

1   I use the term 'older', rather than stating a particular age, because this varies from person to person. Some people feel 'old' at 50, while others more than 80 years of age still do not regard themselves as 'old'.

dying. We[2] believe that using these real life examples will be helpful to others in their journeys too.

Ageing and Dying

Few people, apart from indigenous people, die young these days. In western societies, dying has become much more closely associated with ageing. Many people as they grow older live with chronic illnesses, including heart disease, chronic lung disease and diabetes, to name the most commonly occurring chronic illnesses. (For more information on this, please refer to Appendix I.) Dementia, too, becomes much more common in later life, simply because more people are living longer. As well, frailty is more likely in people aged more than 80 or 90 years of age and may lead to death. At some point in the lifespan of each person, if they have not succumbed to illnesses or conditions, the physical body begins to lose its ability to mend itself, or to replace old cells, and energy levels fall. This is so even though much can be done to maintain good physical health for much longer these days.

So, what do most older people die from?

Most older people die from the effects of chronic diseases, and these are briefly outlined in Appendix II, where the leading causes of death of older people are summarised.

2　The team of Hand, Marston and Seidel-Hooke collected the stories of people who were dying and their loved ones.

FACTORS AFFECTING LONGEVITY

Three main factors influence the longevity of any particular person. First, genetic potential, which the person has inherited from their parents, will influence what is potentially possible. Second, lifestyle plays an important part and is one of the reasons why people are living longer these days. Exercise, good diet, the public health measures that provide us pure water, proper sewerage and good air quality, as well as immunisations against common infections that used to kill many young people, all lead to increased longevity. Education is an important player in this mix, providing people with the knowledge and motivation to lead healthier and longer lives.

WHAT IS SO DIFFERENT ABOUT OLDER PEOPLE DYING?

In comparison with young people and children, more older people are likely to die gradually from complications of one or more chronic diseases. Also, and this is important, expectations of dying and death are different for older people. At one level, older people are expected to die; at another level, death is often unexpected, or its possibility is denied, even in older age – for example, Frank Brennan (2009)[3] tells the story of a daughter who was insistent that her dying mother (95 years of age) not be told she was dying. Later, when the doctor responded to the mother's question to him about dying, she asked him not to tell her daughter: 'My daughter can be a very anxious woman and I am sure she wouldn't cope if she knew that I knew' (Brennan 2009, p.38).

At some stage in the journey towards death, treatment goals will change as the realisation of death becomes more obvious. At this time, the change is from active treatment

---

3   Frank Brennan is a consultant in Palliative Medicine Calvary Health Care, Kogarah, Sydney.

that would be aimed towards cure, to palliation. We often hear the term 'palliative care', but what does it mean?

WHAT IS PALLIATIVE CARE?

Palliative care affirms life and regards dying as a normal process. In recognising this, palliative care neither hastens nor postpones death; it helps provide relief from pain and suffering and offers support to the person and his or her family, encouraging a full and active life for as long as possible (Hudson and O'Connor 2007). Palliative care is for those who are dying not only from cancer, but from any cause. This has been an important extension of the vital work of the palliative care movement in recent years.

Palliative care aims to improve the quality of life for people who have a life-threatening illness, and is defined as:

> an approach that improves the quality of life of patients and their families facing the problem associated with life-threatening illness, through the prevention and relief of suffering by means of early identification and impeccable assessment and treatment of pain and other problems, physical, psychosocial and spiritual. (World Health Organization 2010)

- Palliative care aims to improve quality of life for patients and families through prevention and relief of pain and suffering.
- It is achieved through physical, psychosocial and spiritual care.

While physical, cultural, psychological and social needs have been addressed in palliative care for some decades now, spiritual care has taken longer to be recognised; however, it is now recognised by the World Health Organization as part of holistic care.

Part of the approach to end-of-life issues is to see the context of dying and death. Cousins (1981) wrote: 'Death is not the ultimate tragedy of life. The ultimate tragedy is depersonalisation, dying...separated from the spiritual nourishment that comes from being able to reach out to a loving hand, separated from a desire to experience the things that make life worth living, separated from hope' (p.133). It is important, then, to consider what spirituality is.

WHAT IS SPIRITUALITY? IS IT DIFFERENT FROM RELIGION?

Spirituality is about meaning in life and relationship, and as such it is a critical part of what it is to be human. Some people see religion and spirituality as being the same. Others say that there is no relationship between religion and spirituality. The author of this book maintains that religion and spirituality are connected, but that while some people do not practise a religion, all do have spiritual dimension. Figure I.1 illustrates how ultimate meaning and spirituality are mediated by each person.

Spirituality is about meaning in life and is mediated through:

- relationship (with God and/or others)
- the arts
- the environment or creation
- religion (religion takes in all aspects of spirituality).

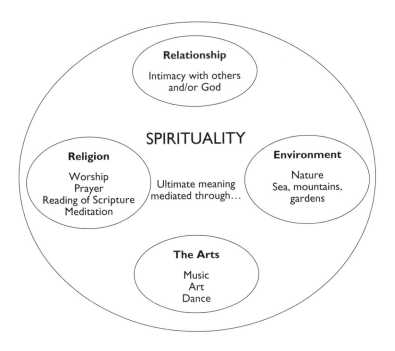

Figure I.1 Ways of mediating the spiritual dimension
Source: MacKinlay 2006, p.14

WHAT IS SPIRITUAL CARE?

Spiritual care is care that addresses the needs of people in their search for meaning in life; it helps them to make sense of their lives and is especially relevant during the journey into death. Spiritual care includes emotional care and is often associated with the provision of pastoral care. However, spiritual care may be given by nurses, doctors, social workers and others, as well as by the traditional providers of spiritual care (the pastoral carers and chaplains).

Spirituality and spiritual care involve issues such as dealing with fear, guilt, forgiveness, grief, finding meaning in the face of death, reconciliation with loved ones, and new beginnings. Spiritual care also involves finding ways of saying thanks, celebrating the good things of life, and affirming important memories and a sense of hope. Designing rituals and symbols that are meaningful for the person who is dying and his or her family are important ways of helping people connect with this process of end-of-life care. The spiritual dimension can also be nourished through religious practices of prayer, Scripture readings, liturgy, services of thanksgiving, sacramental absolution and pronouncement of forgiveness of sins.

PASTORAL CARE

Pastoral care addresses issues of life meaning and the spiritual dimension, often focusing on using listening skills as the pastoral carer accompanies the dying person and his or her family. Pastoral carers do not usually provide specific religious care, unless they also happen to be ordained ministers of their religion, whether Christian, Jewish, Muslim, Hindu or Buddhist. Pastoral carers also provide pastoral and spiritual care for people who do not practise a religion.

Pastoral care is defined as the intentional presence of one person with another in a journey together.

SPIRITUALITY AND RELIGION IN THE PROCESS OF DYING AND DEATH

SPIRITUAL NEEDS

The spiritual needs of a dying person can sometimes be overlooked in the busyness of physical care. However, for those experiencing it, spiritual distress is very real. If we understand spirituality as purpose or core meaning in life and relationship, this provides a starting point for thinking about ways of meeting spiritual needs of those who are facing either their own death or the death of their loved ones. The person who has a clear sense of their meaning and purpose in life will more likely have a sense of peace as he or she approaches death. For some people, becoming aware of their purpose in life is key to facing death with a sense of completion and a life well lived. Some others may face their dying with a sense of things left undone; of relationships to be reconciled, forgiveness to be given or to be sought, and a lack of peace and hope. People who practise a religion may gain great strength at this stage through the rituals, prayers and worship of their community of faith. Even for those without a religion, the use of ritual and symbol is often of great value.

Table I.1 below outlines some of the possible spiritual needs of a dying person (based on Koenig 1994; MacKinlay 2006) and indicates where more in-depth information may be found in this book for some specific needs.

TABLE I.1 SPIRITUAL NEEDS IN THE PALLIATIVE PROCESS

Spiritual need	Desired outcomes in response to spiritual needs in palliative care
For meaning, purpose and hope	To be valued as a person at any particular time and in any circumstances. To have come to know one's own purpose in this life.
To transcend circumstances	To recognise that it is possible to prevail in difficult circumstances (see Chapter 8, 'Transcendence in the Process of Death and Dying').
For support in dealing with loss	To have empathetic others come alongside, and in so doing share the load (see Chapter 1, 'Grief and Loss: A Part of Life').
For continuity	To maintain as much connection with life around as possible. This spiritual need may also include concepts of life after death – of eternal life, or reincarnation, or of living on through one's children, depending on particular beliefs held.
To engage in religious behaviours and receive validation and support of these	Religious beliefs and practices to be practised, respected and actively encouraged and facilitated by others (see Chapter 6, 'Prayer', and Chapter 7, 'Responding to Meaning: Symbol and Ritual').
For personal dignity and sense of worthiness	To be respected as a person of worth and considered in decision-making.
For unconditional love	To feel cherished and loved.

To express anger and doubt	Freedom to speak openly of concerns, including talking about dying and death as is relevant for the particular person and his or her family.
To feel God is on their side	To feel accepted, loved and approved of by God.
To love and serve others	To pass on to others the skills required in dying.
To forgive and be forgiven	To be reconciled with God, self and others (see Chapter 9, 'Healing of Relationships').
To prepare for death	Acceptance and readiness to follow the final life career (see Chapter 3, 'The Final Life Career', and Chapter 4, 'Accepting that Death will Come').

Doing a life review with a focus on spiritual or meaning components can be an important way to identify spiritual needs. By including spiritual aspects in a life review process, persons are able to reflect and search for meaning in their particular life circumstances. They are also able to recall earlier coping mechanisms that can be used again at times of need. Additionally, a person who is dying might still have a strong desire to help others (Steinhauser *et al.* 2000). As death approaches, individuals may reflect about what really matters in their life that they would like to share with others (Lewis 2001). A pastoral care worker or a chaplain is able to assist in that endeavour. Life review is discussed in Chapter 3, 'The Final Life Career'.

Implicit in the table above is the need for each person to be regarded as a unique and whole person, and for a dying person to be treated with integrity (Steinhauser *et al.* 2000). It is also important to relate to the person in the context of the whole of his or her life, as opposed to the person's current situation (Steinhauser *et al.* 2000).

This might entail the sharing of memories with caregivers and perhaps engaging in rituals that have meaning for the dying person. Some of the rituals might be religious; others might be centred more on family occasions, such as a particular way of celebrating a family event.

IS RELIGION ALWAYS HELPFUL FOR A PERSON WHO IS DYING?

As a person who is dying, or family member, you should have access to pastoral care, which can be offered according to your own culture, and/or religious beliefs. If you change your mind and wish for religious support, which previously you have not ever wanted, or have rejected, your wishes must be respected. For people with no religious beliefs, to be badgered by well-meaning religious people is just as distressing as not being offered religious support would be for someone to whom religion is important.

1

GRIEF AND LOSS

A PART OF LIFE

Throughout our lives we experience loss and grief, sometimes in seemingly small ways – for example, the loss of a pet, moving house and the loss of neighbours and friends, changing schools, jobs, and/or communities; yet these are still real experiences in our everyday lives. To some extent, then, we have learned to live with loss. The ways we have used to cope with loss and to grieve have become part of our lives. As we grow older we are, at some level, well prepared by our life experiences to grapple with the larger losses of life; often, however, these losses are of the most significant relationships of our lives.

Grief does not run a set course and disappear; it takes time and we sometimes talk about 'grief work', meaning the work that each of us does as we struggle to come to terms with these largest losses of our lives.

Most of us do not like to think about dying or talk about death, yet it is something that we will all face. The reality of death becomes more apparent as we grow older, not only for ourselves, but also as our loved ones and friends begin to die around us. In the book *Tuesdays with Morrie*, the author, Mitch Albom, a young man, describes a conversation he had with Morrie, his former lecturer, who was now facing death, about growing old. The older man's attitudes are typical of those of a person who has many years of life experience, and has learned what it means to live with a progressive and debilitating disease that will lead to death. Morrie surprises his younger friend by talking of growing older being about growth, not just decrement and decay. He talks, as many older people do, about the real possibilities for growth in the face of dying and death (Albom 1997).

No matter how we look at ageing or death, we will begin to face an array of losses and experience grief as a response to these losses. Grief has been described as the 'process of adjusting to the loss', in which the 'degree of suffering experienced reflects the size of the gap between what is and what is desired' (Mitchell, Murray and Hynson 2008, p.82).

Grief itself is normal and responses can be physical, mental, emotional and/or spiritual ones (Australian Government/NHMRC 2006). Another term often used with grief and loss is 'bereavement' and this relates to the 'loss of a person by death' (Dunne 2004, p.45). No matter where we are in our journey of life, when we face the reality of death, we will begin to grieve for what we have lost.

LOSSES AND THE DYING PERSON

In the palliative care setting, many losses can be experienced by the person who is dying. Some of these include:

- loss of a perceived future
- loss of social interactions with others
- loss of being a normal part of the family, particularly if there is a need of hospital care
- loss of dignity and privacy during treatment
- loss of independence and freedom
- loss of self-esteem.

(Mitchell *et al.* 2008, p.83)

LOSS OF A PERCEIVED FUTURE

As long as we don't know what lies ahead, we can live life as though it is open-ended; being given a diagnosis of impending death, from whatever cause, suddenly changes everything. People will react differently to being told their time is limited. Some will become depressed, while others will find renewed meaning in the life that is still to be lived.

LOSS OF SOCIAL INTERACTIONS WITH OTHERS

Loss of social interaction is often associated with frailty and disability of increasing age – for example, in those more than 85 years of age. Several frail older people have remarked to me[1] that 'life is more precarious now', as they find keeping appointments is harder, and sudden changes in health make it hard to keep up with others. Loss of independence and transport also make it harder to meet with others, and one's circle of friends diminishes.

Energy levels are reduced, and even speaking may take enormous effort for a person who is dying. For some people this loss of social interaction will be an impetus for deepening spiritual awareness and searching for meaning. For others, it may lead to depression.

LOSS OF BEING A NORMAL PART OF THE FAMILY, PARTICULARLY IF THERE IS A NEED OF HOSPITAL CARE

This is quite similar to the loss of social interaction, and often the causes are the same. This loss may also involve physical separation from loved ones and learning to interact with the social settings of hospitals or hospice care. It may result in a sense of remoteness from family

---

1   Comments by older people to Elizabeth MacKinlay.

and what is going on in the world. The way that people respond to these changes varies from person to person.

LOSS OF DIGNITY AND PRIVACY DURING TREATMENT

Many times families have complained about the lack of privacy and dignity for older people as they undergo treatment. Often the person being treated does not have the energy to protest. Heightened staff awareness of the need to preserve dignity of the person is an important aspect of good care. There is no need for loss of dignity. Advocacy is needed to support those who cannot voice their own needs.

LOSS OF INDEPENDENCE AND FREEDOM

This is often seen as a consequence of loss of mobility and the need for various treatments. Pain and suffering may render it impossible for the dying person to be independent. Learning to live within the physical constraints may be challenging, to say the least.

LOSS OF SELF-ESTEEM

This is an outcome of all the other losses in this process of dying. Does it have to be like this? The short answer is 'no'. Too often acute hospital settings do not allow for the conditions needed for suitable care and support of the dying person. Staff may not have enough training in palliative care, or may fail to recognise the dying person and his or her needs for emotional and spiritual support.

LOSSES EXPERIENCED BY FAMILY AND BY CARERS

Carers, too, will experience many losses as they support their loved one. Sometimes carers find the journey even more difficult; there may be a sense of helplessness – of not knowing what to do, of feeling that something should be done, but what? Some of the losses might be the following.

- The relationship between the carer and the person being cared for changes, resulting in loss of intimacy, or greater difficulty in finding intimacy; loss of shared decision-making or the loss of usual activities.

- There may be loss of anticipated future relationship.

- Role reversal may mean there is loss of a mentor or companion.

- Symbolic losses may occur if the person being cared for is no longer able to function as the head of the family.

- Reorganising family roles can often create grief, if one member of the family is expected to take on the role of carer more than others.

- If the role of carer is intense and long-term, there is often a reduction in outside interaction, creating a loss of identity.

- There may be loss of expectations if plans are put on hold (including retirement plans).

- If caring is done in the carer's home, then a loss occurs in relation to surroundings as the home becomes more like a hospital.

(based on Pierce 2006, pp.15–16)

All of these losses can be compounded when the person who is dying and their loved ones cannot talk about dying. Sometimes family members find it just too hard to talk about dying with their loved one. This, of course, means that the person who is dying may also be isolated, with no one to listen to them.

GRIEVING IN ANTICIPATION

Grieving can begin while the dying person is still alive; relationships can change as people involved respond to the perceived loss. Anticipated grief can be strong, on the one hand preparing the person and their loved ones for dying and bereavement, or, on the other hand, preventing them from preparing as denial of the approaching death sets in.

STAGES OF GRIEVING

Depending on the circumstances, the losses experienced by the carer and the person being cared for will vary. However, there is no denying that grief is painful and can affect every part of our lives and our whole being. The five stages of grief identified by Kubler-Ross as denial, anger, bargaining, depression, acceptance, have been valuable in helping people to recognise signs of grief; however, grief does not fit nicely into set stages (Kubler-Ross 1970). We also recognise other common emotions such as guilt, sorrow, anxiety, confusion, sadness, pain and a longing for what is lost (Australian Government/NHMRC 2006).

It used to be said that there were expected periods of grief, and that people moved through these stages in a certain order. Now we know that grief can be unexpected and may arouse deep emotions, even years after the person has died. A grieving person may come to a sense of acceptance, only to move back into one of the other stages and then recycle again. The length of our grief does not relate to the depth of our love for that which is lost (Manning 1991). 'Do not let anyone hurry you (in your grief), and, most of all, do not hurry yourself' (p.18). How long does grief last? The following quotation is from a man who lost his son through a mountain climbing accident some twelve years before; he writes:

> Rather often I am asked whether the grief remains as intense as when I wrote. The answer is, No. The wound is no longer raw. But it has not disappeared. That is as it should be. If he was worth loving, he is worth grieving over. Grief is existential testimony to the worth of the one loved. That worth abides. (Wolterstorff 1987, p.5)

We all grieve at different rates; no one way is better than any other.

Dying and bereaved people need to grieve in their own way and to be affirmed in their grief. We can do this by journeying with the person, to be there to comfort and console, to know when to touch and when not to, and when to be there and when they need solitude. Great sensitivity is needed to walk this journey with people who are dying, their carers and those who are bereaved. It is always hard to face the unknown. The value of being a friend, a companion in their journey, should not be underestimated (Reid 1996).

There is a great deal written about the concept of grief and the various ways it can affect people. We are all unique; therefore, how you experience the range of emotions that may occur will be different for each person. You may also experience physical signs of grief, such as sleep and even memory difficulties. In reality, there are many ways to express grief and many of these are affected by our culture, beliefs, gender, personality, social support and other aspects of our lives.

No matter what you are experiencing, if you are feeling that your grief is getting beyond your ability to cope, then it is worth talking with a doctor, counsellor, spiritual care provider or member of the palliative care team.

The way we express grief is unique; the way we deal with grief is also unique. However, there are some similarities.

Some suggestions to help with grief are:

- share your feelings with trusted friends
- write a poem, letter or journal
- music is often therapeutic
- give yourself permission to cry or to laugh
- ask questions
- draw comfort from memories.

(Wei and Levkoff 2000; Manning 1991)

Wendy[2] found writing her journal to be very therapeutic. She found that she could give herself permission to cry: 'I allow the tears to come and often when least expected.' Wendy and Lewis both found that their faith sustained them through times of anxiety and grief. After church on a Sunday, people would gather around Lewis in his wheelchair and talk about the week. 'It was one of the special times of the week for Lewis. God was very much in our lives. Yes, we continued to grieve in

---

2   Wendy kept a journal of her experience as she journeyed with her husband, Lewis, which she titled *A journey of loving, caring and sharing*.

our own ways and felt sad that an end for one of us was not far away. But until then, we remained positive and grateful for every day and for all the blessings we had experienced and continued to receive.'

Grief is normal. It does not only occur after someone has died but also is found in grieving the losses that occur as death approaches. Grief does not look the same for every person, and ways of coping with that grief will also differ.

2

FEAR OF DYING

Fear of dying is one of the greater fears for humans. We each only die once, and in a death-denying society we are often far removed from others who are dying. The process of dying is often both denied and private. Most people are less afraid of death than they are of the process of dying (MacKinlay 2001). This is particularly so for older people. It is fear that may prevent people being able to talk about dying and, therefore make it hard to include loved ones in the journey. This fear is felt not only by people who are facing their own dying, and their families; it is also felt by staff of aged care facilities. One study (MacKinlay 2006) found that staff working in aged care were reluctant to raise the topic of death and dying with those they cared for. Yet, when they did a short interview containing questions about dying and death with people they had cared for over a long time, they found that these people did want to speak about dying and death.[1]

---

[1] Nurses asked elderly residents about their hopes and fears about dying and death. The nurses were amazed that the residents seemed eager to talk about these subjects. Some said it was like opening the floodgates. It helped the nurse to get to know the people they cared for better. Older people remarked that they had never been asked questions like these before, and they readily engaged in the conversations.

THE RELUCTANCE TO TALK ABOUT DEATH AND DYING

Why is there reluctance to speak of death and dying? First, many people do not know how to speak of death and dying. For young people, death might seem a long way off; however, for older people, there may be a gradual realisation that they have already lived the greater part of their lives. Dying is the last part of life, termed by some the final life career (Kimble 2003). While many older people, having witnessed their spouse and peers die, are familiar with death and dying, this does not make the process easier. To a great extent, their life experiences influence the way they view their own mortality. One older woman expressed this apprehension of losing control and not knowing what might lie ahead when she said, 'I don't like to be off my legs or lose my mind' (MacKinlay 2001, p.143).[2] An older person wishing to talk about dying with friends and relatives may find there is a reluctance for friends and family to engage in this conversation. It is useful to understand why this might be.

In contemporary western society the subject of death and dying has been denied or avoided over the past century, as death has been gradually removed from the intimacy of the home to institutions, especially hospitals (Stevens, McFarlane and Stirling 2000). Denial and avoidance can take many forms. Possibly the primary form originates from the fact that many lives today are prolonged by medical means, which promotes the ideas that, in any circumstance, something more can always be done and that disease can be cured (Shuman 2003). This has been called the medicalisation of death, where ageing and dying are treated as diseases to be defeated by medical technology (Shuman 2003).

---

2   This older woman feared physical or mental disabilities of later life.

Another form of denying death is the adoption of language (Kastenbaum 2000) such as 'passed away' or 'slipped away'. Relatives and friends of those who are dying are often challenged by their own mortality if they speak of dying. They might also prefer not to speak of dying because of a misguided, but genuine, desire not to distress the older person. As well, death is often reported on the television and radio in a manner remote from human emotion. That can promote an attitude of detachment and sometimes indifference to death. Another contributing factor to the societal attitude of denying death is the way that young people are admired and the elderly devalued (Stevens *et al.* 2000).

FEAR OF THE UNKNOWN, FEAR OF BEING VULNERABLE

This is a common human fear. There remains a sense of mystery about death; none of us has experienced it personally, before facing our own dying and death. In a society that places great emphasis on autonomy and independence, being vulnerable is frightening. Among frail older people in nursing homes, interviewed in depth (MacKinlay 2006), few found the actual experience of being vulnerable as frightening as they had imagined. This may be helpful for us to know, as often the actual experience is not as bad as fear of the unknown that might lie ahead. It is also hard for us to imagine what an experience is like for a loved one, when all we can do is to look on. Often it seems harder for the one who watches.

3

THE FINAL LIFE CAREER

IS THIS ONLY A TIME OF
WAITING FOR DEATH? OR IS
THERE SOMETHING MORE?

For people who are dying, and their loved ones, the thought of hospice care may present a sense of simply waiting until death. For older people admitted to nursing homes, there may be a similar sense of the impending end of life; nursing homes have been called 'God's Waiting Room' by some; such is the sense of waiting for death. But is that all there is? As death has been removed from the sphere of the private home to institutional settings over the last century, we seem to have lost our sense of intimacy in the process and so much that used to be part of ways of dying has been largely forgotten in the busyness of the early twenty-first century.

This last stage of life is every bit as important as all that has gone before.

THIS MAY BE THE LAST STAGE OF LIFE BUT IT IS STILL IMPORTANT

In fact it can be said that, in dying, there is one more career of life left to live: the final life career. It is only as we personally face the fact that we are each on a journey into death, no matter how we will eventually die, that we can begin to grasp the final meaning of our life. Heinz (1994) has used the term 'final life career' to describe this last part of life. How long does it last? The length of the final life career varies enormously, from years down to months, weeks, or sometimes even less. For some people who have a terminal illness, cancer of some type, or perhaps dementia, the time can vary greatly.

The words: 'Live till you die' really mean that. A friend of mine, having been diagnosed with dementia, remarked that life suddenly became very much more valuable to her. She did not want to miss any of life's experiences. The way we face this final life career will influence the meaningfulness of the journey we make. Our traditions of dying and death in western societies over the twentieth century have largely ignored the possibility of this final stage of life. It is possible that the journey into death can become a positive, fulfilling, albeit challenging journey.

There are two parts to the final life career:

- to hand over to the next generation
- to die well.

HANDING ON THE BATON

There are important things to hand over to the coming generation: our knowledge and wisdom of life and, most important of all, the knowledge of who we are, the story that both forms our identity, and is linked with the identity of our families.

Facing the process of dying and recognising a final phase of life can be an important and precious part of life as a whole (MacKinlay 2006). Finding the final life meanings can take on new importance in the face of dying.

HANDING ON TO COMING GENERATIONS

As humans, we each have a unique life story, and we are part of the stories of our family; for Christians, Jews and Muslims, we are also part of the story of our faith communities and the larger story that goes back to the beginning of time and links us with God. In societies that are multicultural and multi-faith, we acknowledge and affirm the diversity of older people and the particular aspects of preparing for death. Regardless of any faith perspective, all humans seek to find meaning in life, and when coming to the end of life, the questions of life meaning are likely to emerge.

Handing on the baton to the coming generation is an important task of this final life journey. The links between the generations are important. Some questions that may emerge for us are: What does it mean to be a member of my family? What are the values that have been held in tradition for family members over preceding generations? These are important connections to hand on. There has been a tendency in recent decades to think, first, that the story of the older person was not important, and second, that younger people did not want or need to hear the story, based on the assumption that the next generation needed to make its own way in the world. Effective connections across the generations are important in the meaning of our lives and the lives of those we love.

My [Anne Hand's] mother was recently moved into a nursing home after having a stroke. Her long-term memory is still intact, although she is now quite confused over her immediate needs and daily happenings. However, when she was shown photos from her past, she was able to tell stories and name those in the photos like they were taken yesterday. Her two adult granddaughters delighted in seeing their grandmother as a young woman and to hear stories of the family from previous generations. It was invaluable for them to see their grandmother, not only as a frail, elderly lady, but as a person that has lived a full and enriching life.

FACING THE FINAL LIFE JOURNEY

For each of us a time will come, unless we die very suddenly and unexpectedly, when we will need to face the possibility of our own death. In later life this realisation may come through a diagnosis of a life-threatening illness, or through a slowly progressing frailty or stroke, or dementia. In each situation it will be necessary to face the diagnosis and regroup and reprioritise plans for the future.

Wendy walked this journey towards death with her husband, who finally died at home, receiving palliative care. Wendy recounts the early days of diagnosis and beginning the journey.

Back in May 1999 both my husband, Lewis, and I were awaiting results of tests for possible cancer. We had led busy and active lives with few worries. My result for breast cancer proved to be none other than a speck of powder on my skin when the X-ray was taken. However, for Lewis the result was positive for prostate cancer. Despite the initial tears on my part, and probable worries by Lewis (which he kept to himself) we learned that this could be treated with hormone (Zoladex) injections three-monthly. At more than $1,200 each these expensive injections were paid for by Department of Veteran Affairs, as Lewis had a veteran's gold card. We had heard that prostate cancer in older men is usually very slow and that Lewis would probably die of something else. Hormone therapy is usually given when the cancer has spread beyond the prostate gland but in Lewis's case, it was decided to use it earlier. So our life together continued as normal except for sexual relations (erectile dysfunction) as Lewis was unable to maintain an erection – this can happen after radiation. But marriage to us was much more than sex.

Despite the prostate cancer, from the age of 81 until the age of 85 Lewis did volunteer work as a trucking off-sider for Anglicare. He continued to travel both in Australia, usually camping, and overseas. We have a photo of him on the back of a motorbike in Cambodia just before his 85th birthday. Lewis finished his volunteer work on the truck the day before he encountered problems due to prostate cancer – blocked urethra. It was 13 December 2006.

Lewis and I had entered the last stages of our life together. As Lewis's health deteriorated in the following months, he did not want to go to hospital, and his wishes were respected as much as possible, and I was committed to caring for him at home.

Wendy's journey with Lewis was exactly that: a journey. The excerpt above speaks of the time of diagnosis and early years after that. Certainly, this was well before the time of need for palliative care. As can be seen, they shared a number of years of positive ageing together.

Another story of the journey of life into the process of dying and death is that of Gabrielle. Gabrielle had worked with us at our Centre for Ageing and Pastoral Studies, bringing valuable pastoral care skills, especially the ability to work pastorally with people who have lost their ability to speak through dementia. She wrote the following reflection after having neurosurgery for an inoperable brain tumour.

Just two weeks ago, I was being CAT-scanned for brain tumours. How one's life can be turned upside-down in two weeks.

The brain is so fascinating – here it is affecting my speech, spelling and adding up – all of which I love.

No one knows what the future will hold – how much I must try to concentrate on one day at a time and not look into the future unnecessarily.

I find myself worrying about the future and pull myself back to a day at a time, remembering that I will be given the strength I need to face each stage.

I've been thinking about the 'redemptive power of suffering'. What do I do with this? Where do I put it? I think of Viktor Frankl's words about the attitude to suffering. I can see it's not just for me. Does it do something to bring about some sort of balance, equilibrium? I believe it is the price we pay for the precious gift of free will – and an opportunity to bring God's passion and compassion to the world. Maybe it's about me joining my radiotherapy 'crown of thorns' to that of Jesus.

CHANGE OF PERSPECTIVE: TO LIVE ONE DAY AT A TIME

Gabrielle at this stage was grappling with coming to terms with her diagnosis and, wisely, endeavouring to live one day at a time. In any critical time of our lives, time seems to be reduced to the immediate. Gabrielle had worked so closely with people who had trouble with finding the right words to speak, and she now experienced these same things. And like many people with dementia, she was very aware of what was happening. It was helpful for her to be able to write and reflect on what was happening.

Yet another example of a person facing death, this time through living with a chronic and slowly progressive disease, was Morrie Schwartz. This is a moving story of a young man and what he learns as he accompanies his professor in this final life journey. In Morrie's final days, reflected in the book *Tuesdays with Morrie* (Albom 1997), he talks to the young man, Mitch Albom, about death and dying. Morrie speaks of the uncertainty of the dying process; some people have talked of unpredictability. At one point Morrie tells his young friend that he doesn't think he will live to see the new day. Then he describes the most unexpected feeling he had of peace when he woke in the morning, peace at the idea of dying. He describes it as a kind of acceptance of the fact that dying is inevitable. At this stage, Morrie seems to recognize the importance of love, even at this time of dying, and the need to make peace with those we love. Like many others, Morrie recognizes that death ends a life but the relationship still continues, although in a changed form, for those still living.

WALKING THE JOURNEY WITH SOMEONE WHO IS DYING: A MIDWIFE FOR THE DYING

Being with someone as they die is one of the most important things we can do for another person. This is a concept of being a midwife for the dying. As we need someone to accompany us into life, so it is also for the final journey into death. Walking this final journey in life with the one dying is a special role for those privileged to be a part of this journey.

This is a sacred time, and a time that does not fit well within the goals of an acute health care setting. Essentially, to die is not only a biological process; for each person, death is also a unique and a spiritual journey. Medicalisation of the dying process has largely removed death from the intimacy of family and friends; there is a need to reclaim the spiritual dimension so that people are not isolated in their dying. Humans are by nature meaning makers, and core meaning is a spiritual concept. Finding meaning becomes more important in later life, and especially in the final career of life.

OUR LIFE STORY: MEANING AND IDENTITY THROUGH STORY

Story is important to all of us; it is tied up with who we are and what we see as important in life. It is often only as we grow older, or face a life-threatening condition, that we are suddenly brought up against the questions: Why am I here? What is the meaning and purpose of my life? These are deep and spiritual questions and go to the heart of what it means to be human. Viktor Frankl, the Jewish psychiatrist who wrote the book *Man's Search for Meaning*

(Frankl 1984), which involved his reflection of experiences as an inmate of World War II concentration camps, wrote that it is only as we face death that we are able to see the whole meaning of our lives.

This is a time when it is possible, perhaps for the first time, to reminisce and reflect on our life journey and the meaning that we find in our life. Each life is precious and unique; each person will have different and unique life experiences and will have responded to life in his or her own way. No one can make our life meanings for us; they are uniquely ours. But others form an important part of the networks and relationships in the lives of each person. We often talk about being autonomous human beings, but that is largely illusion, as we need the human contact and support of others in our lives. We are really not autonomous but interdependent beings!

LIFE REVIEW AND SPIRITUAL REMINISCENCE

Life review is done by many people as a natural part of growing older. There are times when this process becomes much more important, especially when someone becomes aware that their life is nearing its end. An important function of life review is to find meaning and purpose in one's life. Life review becomes important with this realisation of the nearness of death. There is a growing interest in society, for many people, in searching to find their roots. The TV program 'Who do you Think you Are?' awakens interest in tracing our family history. In many families, someone takes on the responsibility to find the family history and bring it together. Too often, however, in the busyness of this world, families have not had time to sit together to tell and listen to the story.

> Life review, spiritual reminiscence, narrative – whatever you call it – it is all important in connecting us with each other and our identity.

The process of reminiscence, and in fact, spiritual reminiscence, where the story focuses on the meaning of the life journey, not just the facts of what events occurred and when, is a very valuable process that can bring a sense of hope, completion and meaning to the lives of both the person who is dying and their wider family. The process can be facilitated in a number of ways. For those who are listeners, this can be privileged time. The story may be spoken, it may be recorded, it may be written; it is a gift from one generation to the next. To be effective, the story needs to be told and needs to be heard, so that there is the need for both the storyteller and the story listener.

THE UNFOLDING OF STORY

Given the opportunity, many people will find telling their story to be a special time and the very telling of the story can also be deeply nourishing for those who listen.

What kinds of questions work best? Is it just remembering the 'old days?' It seems to have deeper meaning than that. If the story is not told until the person is very near to death, he or she may not have a lot of energy to speak, and it may need to be told in parts, with time between, as the person has energy. How often have you heard it said 'If only we had heard the story from Aunt Jessie, or Uncle Reg'...? The story is important for others to hear too.

Recording the family tree is one part of the story, but there is much more. That is the general family story, but there is also the unique story of the individual person that links with the stories of other family members. Each person's story is told from their view of life and is unlike any other. We sometimes hear it said that 'the way Betty tells her story is not the same as the way her cousin tells it.' In fact, it can't be the same story, as it is seen from a different viewpoint. In the Christian Gospels, all four of the writers have recorded much of the same material, but they have also contributed differences of emphasis and details in telling the story from their own unique view of 'what happened'. This actually brings richness to the main story; it helps us to understand the different perspectives and build a larger picture. So it is with our own stories. We are not simply wanting a 'true' account when we hear or read a personal life review. We are looking at the person and how their life experiences have shaped their lives and their relationships. There are joys, hopes, disappointments, grief, guilt, anger, forgiveness and love woven through each person's life. There are the remembrances of achievements and also the remembrances of loss of loved ones through death or separation.

There are numbers of books written on narrative, life review and spiritual reminiscence that may be helpful to read in putting together ways of sharing the life story (Birren and Cochran 2001; Gibson 2004; Kenyon *et al.* 2001; Morgan 2002).

A number of questions can help guide the telling of story. These are very broad questions that help to call forth the depths of life meaning. Authors Kenyon, Clark and de Vries (2001) say that we *are* story, and indeed, our very identity is bound up in story. Spiritual reminiscence is valuable in assisting people to reach a sense of final life meaning.

Some questions that may help guide the story are:

- What gives greatest meaning to your life now?
    - What is most important in your life?
    - What keeps you going?
    - Is life worth living?
    - If life is worth living – why is it worth living? If not – why not?
- Looking back over your life:
    - What do you remember with joy?
    - What do you remember with sadness?
- What are the hardest things for you now?
- What do you look forward to now?

(based on MacKinlay 2006)

These questions will work for people of different cultures and faiths. More specific questions will include the particular religious faith of the person.

THE FINAL JOURNEY: CARE PERSPECTIVES

The final life journey calls for the most holistic of all care to enable the person to die as he or she wishes, and to support them in their struggles. For health providers and pastoral carers and chaplains, this means using all one's senses and assessments to enable the person to find meaning, peace and completion in their final journey.

Sometimes older people just ask God to 'take them', and if this has not happened – why doesn't this happen? St Paul longed to be at home with the Lord, but found that he still had life to live before that time came. 'So we do not lose heart. Even though our outer nature is wasting away, our inner nature is being renewed day by day' (2 Corinthians 4:16). And, further: 'Yes, we do have confidence, and we would rather be away from the body and at home with the Lord. So whether we are at home or away, we make it our aim to please him' (2 Corinthians 5:8–9). Can we be in charge of the time of our going? I think we can, to some extent. Fear is the greatest barrier to dying well. Sometimes it seems that the person who is dying wants to die and can see no reason to continue to live, and yet, for some reason, holds onto life, not ready to 'let go'.

I have a sense of this final life journey being one of 'letting go'. Until we are able and ready to let go of life, we will continue to seem to 'hang on' and not die. This is a deeply spiritual experience, and I am sure that many of you have either known this or have heard of situations where a dying person stayed alive, against all the odds, until someone important to them came to them, or until they had completed some unfinished business. Then, often, a person will die within a very short time.

For those who care for the dying person, part of the process is being able to support and affirm the dying person. In a very real sense this is certainly a spiritual journey. The answer to the question: 'Why doesn't God take me?' is not, 'God will take you when you (or God) are ready.' Rather, it is to assist the person to be reconciled and accepting of their life, to reach a sense of peace and rightness about their life, so that they may be truly ready to die. This may perhaps be through telling their story and coming to a sense of the story's completion. It may be through a sense of having achieved all that they wanted to, of having lived in significant relationships, lived to see children and grandchildren and perhaps even great-grandchildren born, grow up and do well in life. Of course there are times when things have not gone as hoped or planned, and it is a task of preparing for the final life career to bring together all these parts of the tapestry of life and see the whole of one's life for the first time. It is then that the purpose of that person's life may finally become apparent. Sometimes the person who is dying may be so caught up in fear, and perhaps bitterness, that this sense of peace will not come, and that makes for a very hard death. Resolution may come through making amends for something from the past. It may be through saying 'goodbye' to someone important. Whatever the situation, it is when these things are completed that the person will be ready to die.

HOPE – DESPAIR

Hope is one side of the picture, the other is despair. What leads to hope? There is something deep within the human being that longs for hope. What do older people who are dying hope for? This can vary a great deal. Some older people hope to be reconciled with loved ones. It is surprising how many have lost contact with one or more family members, or have resentful feelings towards others. Being right with family members is an important part of this final life journey. Now, with so many more blended families, this may become even more complicated.

Numbers of older people hold strong beliefs that they will be reunited through death with loved ones who have died before them. For Christians there is hope of life eternal. In Jewish terms, hope is maintained through religious practices, scriptures, and traditions based in the culture of the community. Islam involves belief in God and the hereafter, a moral and ethical code by which to live, and through human relationships. Jews, Christians and Muslims all find hope in the one God. Hindu and Buddhist beliefs assert the continuity of life, so that hope can be found in the continuing cycle of life, death and renewed life (MacKinlay 2010). For numbers of older people there is uncertainty as to what shape this afterlife may take. People facing their death may wish to explore the possibilities of life after death in discussion with a chaplain or pastoral carer, or with their own minister. Some may be hesitant to ask questions. It should be clear that these questions are legitimate ones to ask. No questions should be off limits at this stage.

Members of different faiths and also those who have no religious background may wish to ask questions and talk about the meaning of death. Resource people of their own religious faith, or a person who can hear their story, should be available to meet with the dying person where this is desired. This resource person could be a pastoral carer, a chaplain, a nurse, a trained volunteer, or a friend. In many respects the important part of this role is to be present to the dying person, to listen and reflect, to respect and to care. A resource on multi-faith issues around ageing and dying in different cultures and religions is the book *Ageing and Spirituality across Faiths and Cultures* (MacKinlay 2010).

4

ACCEPTING THAT DEATH WILL COME

Often it is difficult to grasp the reality of the approach of death. Gabrielle, who had worked pastorally with many people who were dying, when faced with her own dying prepared an outline of what she would like for the funeral service some eight months prior to her death. On the other hand, Wendy and Lewis certainly experienced the difficulty of grasping this reality in the early stages, as they were struggling with coming to terms with the changes in lifestyle and prognosis. We sometimes think that, once the person has been told of his or her diagnosis, he or she will take it on board and move forward on the basis of having been told. Sometimes, however, it is not that simple. People tend to hear what they can cope with at the time. Sometimes they do not 'hear' because they are not ready. Wendy has words of her experience of this with Lewis.

Initially Lewis was in denial of his gradual deterioration due to his illness. Even after hearing that the prostate cancer was rare and aggressive, Lewis still expected to recover, or at least return to his previous physical condition. He had had a blocked urethra, urethra catheter, radiation, major infection, temporarily blocked kidneys, SPC (suprapubic catheter) inserted and a rebore (TURPS – trans urethral resection of the prostate gland). Notwithstanding keeping the patient's needs to the fore, there came a time when it had to be said: 'Didn't you hear Dr say that your cancer is rare and aggressive?' After this initial denial period came some downers (not really depression, but on the way to it) and then, with acceptance (but never discussed between us), the old quality of life resurfaced. The home-based palliative care nurse said to me that, as the carer, I needed to take hold of situations (referring to a specific matter). As a word of reassurance, when you know the patient really well you will know when it is appropriate, or even time to take control.

DECISIONS ALONG THE WAY

For any person approaching death, changes keep coming, in energy levels, in pain and discomforts, and what is possible at the particular stage of the journey. It is always important to keep the motto of 'living until you die' clearly in mind, as there may be times when it is hard, but at other times there is a reprieve, and time and space to do and be together and enjoy, as Wendy describes.

Six months on, and again the daily routine changed considerably. Both Lewis and I had accepted that this was our last journey together, although he still would not talk about death. We acknowledged to each other that we would take things day by day. My activities were restricted, but I continued with my music and an occasional massage and a walk most days. There was an acceptance of the situation, which allowed us both to relax. When I suggested cancelling all specialist appointments and X-rays there was a sigh of relief from Lewis. He really didn't want much medical interference, just enough to keep him comfortable. We said no to hospital hydration and to having oxygen at home for his sleep apnoea.

I had already planned Lewis's funeral and celebration of his life services. To have the time to plan this carefully, as he would have liked it, was a real blessing. Lewis was not aware of this, nor would he have wanted to know.

WHAT DOES IT MEAN TO DIE WELL?

One of the factors in dying well, for many, is the need to feel in control. Research has indicated that the most important characteristic of a good death, for patients, caregivers and professionals, is that it be pain-free (Steinhauser *et al.* 2000). This topic is addressed in further detail in Chapter 5, 'Pain, Distress and Suffering'.

In situations that are often difficult to predict and/ or control, a sense of control can be provided through collaborative decisions made and followed by all the partners in care: the family, the person who is dying, and health care providers. Another component of a good death is that clear communication in decision making exists between the patient, family and physicians (Steinhauser *et al.* 2000). Decisions need to be made before a time of crisis arises, and these decisions need to be clearly articulated. The use of ambiguous language can cause miscommunication. For example, a doctor might not clearly communicate the clinical expectations of outcomes for a patient, using words such as 'may not improve' instead of 'is dying' (Ellershaw and Ward 2003). That can lead to important decisions being postponed or not addressed at all.

Some factors in a good death are:

- to feel the time is right – sense of life completion
- to have come to final life meanings
- to be comfortable, pain-free and to have symptoms well managed
- to be reconciled to others
- to have handed over the story to the next generation.

TIME AND OPPORTUNITY TO PREPARE FOR DEATH

From the perspective of the dying person and their caregiver, the time and opportunity to prepare for death is seen as an important concept in experiencing a 'good death' (Wilkes 1998).

Being able to acknowledge that death is imminent is clearly helpful for an older person who is dying (Gott *et al.* 2008). However, as so many people are uncomfortable talking about death, it may not be possible to acknowledge the nearness of death. Communication about dying and death within a family might be anywhere on a continuum between completely open and completely closed (Lugton 2003). Only the family members can know what is acceptable in their family. For example, some families regard sensitivity to others' feelings to include not speaking plainly about death and dying. Cultural issues may be important here. In this instance, any discussion might be viewed as upsetting for the older person and therefore avoided. Open communication within the family about dying and death facilitates the process of end-of-life care; it opens as the possibility of asking questions and putting plans in place; affairs may be put in order and funeral plans made. Open communication provides opportunities for reconciliation and for saying goodbye.

DYING IN HOSPICE, AGED CARE FACILITY, OR HOSPITAL

Ninety percent of deaths in Australia today happen in institutions, nursing homes and hospitals (Stevens *et al.* 2000), while 83 percent of deaths of older people in the UK occur in hospitals and care homes (Ahmad and O'Mahony 2005). However, this does not mean that these are the best places to die, nor that real choices have been made about the best place to die. Hospitals are set up for the active treatment of people who are ill or having surgery or other medical procedures; they are not planned for providing a peaceful setting in which to die. Often a last-minute race to hospital results in a great deal of unnecessary distress for a dying person and their family. A hospital is busy, with no place for the waiting and final journey, and for families to be together. On the other hand, a hospice is designed to be a place where people can prepare for death and live as near normal a life as possible until they die. The atmosphere of a hospice is designed to provide quiet and peace, with an emphasis on holistic care. Aged care facilities are also planned to be more home-like than hospitals.

When a person is dying, there is no good reason for taking them to hospital to die. If there is the need for urgent life-saving treatment, that is different, but life-saving treatment would not be appropriate for a person who is dying. During the dying process, the goals have changed from life-saving to supporting the person in a peaceful and pain-free death.

WHAT ABOUT DYING AT HOME?

If, as stated above, 90 percent of deaths occur in hospitals, that might seem to be saying that it might be risky to choose to die at home, but that is not so. Probably about 40 years ago, I witnessed a dear friend of mine die at home. She was cared for through the Peter McCallum Clinic in Melbourne. As a registered nurse, I had witnessed many deaths in hospitals, and in this instance, to be part of my friend's dying over a number of months at home was a special experience for me, allowing me to see the process of dying in a whole new way. Her pain was well managed, her other symptoms were well controlled, and she had adequate back-up from the clinic by nurses who gave excellent care. How good it was for her to have some control over her life, how good it was for her to be with her husband and to be able to have friends in to visit when she wanted.

In Wendy's experience, having Lewis at home worked well.

At times I had some nagging doubts whether treating Lewis at home was the best decision. I often visited an elderly lady in a nursing home who did not have as many or severe medical problems that Lewis had, but because she yelled out in her sleep, she was often still in bed when I visited, unwashed for the day, in a drug-induced sleep, in a darkened room with the door shut. Her room was at the end of corridor. She did not have the quality of life that Lewis had at home. Of more concern, with the rotation of nurses, she saw people she didn't know looking after her. I took action to correct some of this. But it made me realise that, in deciding to care for Lewis at home, I had made the right decision.

A person's wish to die at home may be fulfilled because:

- the person and their family wish to have the person die at home
- there is enough emotional and physical support to remain at home
- palliative care services can be engaged at home.

Dying at home assumes that the above points are able to be addressed, and that the carer is able to act as an advocate for the person dying. It's sometimes hard to be an advocate, as the caregivers have to really know the person and their desires, so that they can be very clear about what they think the person wants and needs. This is evident in the following excerpt from a study by Phillips and Reed (2010) of caregivers of people who were dying:

No matter what, he was not going to a nursing home. He was not going to a hospice facility. I knew my dad. He's old fashioned and his Italian culture – they want to die at home. I knew that my dad wanted to die at home. I don't remember if we ever talked about it, but I knew in my mind that it was what he wanted. It was the right thing. (p.208)

A person's wish to die at home might not eventuate because:

- symptoms become too difficult to control at home
- the carer becomes exhausted and/or anxious
- a belief is held by the patient and/or family that they will get better care in a hospital, or that 'something else can be done'.

In many instances home-based palliative care can deal effectively with any of these issues, except for the case of a carer who becomes exhausted. Again, it is emphasised that acute hospitals are not set up to care for people who are dying.

The concepts of a good death presented here are not exhaustive. The dying person is probably the only person who can define what, for him or her, constitutes a good death. Most likely the optimal circumstance would be that the dying person feels that the time is right to die and feels a sense of completion over a life well lived.

A 'good death' can be made up of many different components, but only the person dying can truly decide what is needed for his or her 'good death'.

Deena Metzger, reflecting on her own anticipated death, wrote:

What I ask from my death, is that at the last minute I will be able to look back over my life and know, without any doubt, the entire story I have been living... Then I will know, despite pain, disappointment, and limitation, that this life of mine has been a good and meaningful work. (Metzger 1993, p.137)

A good death surely must be about having a sense of completion of one's purpose in life. In a recent in-depth interview with a woman who has dementia, I asked where she found meaning in life. She began with these words: 'I've had a good life, I love this world and all creation, and I can feel God's presence so much more lately [she paused], I think it won't be long before I die' (MacKinlay 2006, p.197).

These responses suggest that questions surrounding the topic of death are on the minds of at least some elderly people.

5

PAIN, DISTRESS AND SUFFERING

EFFECTIVE PAIN AND SYMPTOM MANAGEMENT

The focus of this book is not on physical issues, but pain is such an important topic that it must be included in any discussion around dying. Research has indicated that the most important characteristic of a good death for patients, caregivers and professionals is that it be pain-free. Wendy's experience raises some of the practical issues of pain in this process.

We had regular contact with a palliative care nurse every two weeks, initially just by phone, but later they came out weekly. I found these nurses a source of valuable information. They introduced us to slow release pain control, bridging pain release and frequency, and alerted us to having suitable support equipment, as well as pain and nausea injections, plus doctor's authority for future need. What was most reassuring was that they would set up a mini-hospital in the home when the time came. Lewis did not want to go to hospital and his wish was respected. At a later date the palliative care doctor took over some of Lewis's treatment, especially with pain.

Pain relief is an important component of palliative care. To get it right, a team approach is needed; the person who is dying is central to this, but family, carers and health professionals all need to be involved.

FEAR OF PAIN

Many myths are still held regarding pain and its management, and fear of pain remains one of the main causes of anxiety. Pain management has now become a specialty area of practice, and palliative care protocols enable effective management of physical pain. Any negative experiences should be explored with a trusted professional, a doctor or nurse, to enable the fears to be addressed (Lugton 2003). With regular monitoring of the patient's condition and comfort level, good symptom control, including pain and agitation, can be maintained (Ellershaw and Ward 2003).

Dr Frank Brennan, a palliative care physician, addresses the common myths of pain in cancer care; first, he says, in his practice he has never seen a patient who became addicted to morphine; and second, if pain is sufficiently severe to require opioids,[1] they should be used at that point. The use of opioids should be proportionate to the level of pain, not the extent of the illness, and he notes 'that opioids carefully and appropriately used do not precipitate death prematurely' (Brennan and Dash 2009, p.8).

---

1   Opioids are types of pain-relieving drugs, of which morphine is the most used in cancer pain.

Michael Barbato notes that 'Even when unconscious, a person can still perceive pain and appropriate medication must be continued if pain is to be avoided' (Barbarto 2002, pp.23–24). He also notes, like Frank Brennan, that the dose given should be the lowest needed to relieve pain, even though this may need to be a large dose in some situations. Staff in a hospital or residential setting routinely make and record the progress of patients and this practice can be also be organised for those living in the community. Accounts of pain must be taken seriously.

Wendy shares her experience of pain management with her husband living at home:

Even though the pain-relief drugs made it difficult for Lewis to remember things, at other times we had very good communication. Keeping Lewis comfortable and at home worked.

Other symptoms, such as depression, dryness of the mouth, vomiting, nausea, constipation, diarrhoea and dyspnoea (a distressing shortness of breath) can be relieved and managed (Linton and Lach 2007).

There were some problems initially with nausea and vomiting because of Lewis's pain medication. Lewis would take the occasional Maxolon tablet to prevent this occurring. However, when the pain medication increased, he needed to take a Maxolon tablet half an hour before every meal. These tablets also prevented Lewis's history of hiccups reoccurring. This happened during the last four months of his life.

THE PAIN OF SUFFERING

It has been suggested by numbers of researchers that spiritual and existential issues can influence the progress of disease (Mako, Galek and Poppito 2006). One issue that is foremost in people's minds is pain; in many instances pain is due to physical problems, but sometimes it is from existential or spiritual sources and may be related to suffering. Sometimes existential pain is termed 'spiritual distress'. In fact, spiritual pain may be experienced as physical or psychological symptoms (Mako *et al.* 2006, p.1107).

SUFFERING AND PAIN

It is helpful to understand just what is meant by the term 'suffering'. Kestenbaum (2001), writing of healing and Jewish concepts of pain, makes an important distinction in the understanding of pain and suffering. He writes:

> Suffering is a response to pain; it results from the emotional and spiritual meaning that the pain has in one's life. Medicine treats pain; caregiving responds to suffering. (p.5)

Kestenbaum notes that the point at which a situation becomes unbearable is not usually due to an increase in pain, but rather, has to do with the level of suffering. He notes estrangement or separation as a core component of this suffering. Kestenbaum describes the experience of an elderly woman feeling the loss of her role as a mother when she has to be cared for by her family, saying she finds it 'unbearably painful to be suddenly forced into a reversal of roles' (p.6).

The pain of suffering may arise from grief, guilt, resentment, or even anguish; these are experienced at a psychological or spiritual level. Health care providers are becoming more aware of these possibilities. In a study done by Mako *et al.* (2006), a very high proportion (96%) of patients reported having spiritual pain; this was regardless of whether the person held a religious belief system or not. Spiritual pain was reported in three main ways:

- first, as psychological conflict (mainly despair or resignation)
- second, as relationship loss (mainly isolation) or conflict
- third, in relation to the divine (almost equally resignation or despair and anxiety).

It is noted that this study was only of people with cancer in palliative care, however, the findings may be of value for other people who are facing death from other causes.

People reported spiritual pain differently according to their own backgrounds, beliefs and cultures. It is therefore important to consider the origins of pain and suffering when thinking about how pain can be relieved.

Anxiety and depression are also not uncommonly experienced by patients who are dying. The kinds of things that people who are dying find distressing vary, but comments from participants in one study included pain, or the distress of needing to leave home and/or family (Mako *et al.* 2006). In the same study, simply needing someone to listen to one's story was a frequent request made to chaplains. The researchers also noted an overlap at times between depression and spiritual pain.

WHAT IS EXISTENTIAL PAIN LIKE?

How do people describe this kind of pain? Some descriptions are: 'a deep ache in the heart', 'explosion in the body' or 'all over physical pain', or a sense of despair (Mako *et al.* 2006, p.1110). This study found that when physical pain had been relieved with drugs such as morphine, it was then that spiritual pain could be recognised and addressed. So the drugs used to relieve physical pain may serve to highlight the presence of spiritual pain. Spiritual pain will not be relieved by medications because this pain is associated with 'detaching from life and loved ones' (Mako *et al.* 2006, p.1110). This recent understanding of the pain of dying is important for helping those who are dying, their carers and families to understand and cope with the process of dying.

6

PRAYER

The idea of prayer will vary for each person depending on culture, belief and/or personal experience. When faced with dying and death, you may find prayer to be a natural and familiar response. Or you may find, for the first time in your life, that you have a desire or need to pray. For still others, prayer has not been and still is not the way that they would respond to facing their dying and death.

Prayer can be described as an earnest request or a conversation with God and originates in a relationship with God. A conversation assumes that there is talking and listening on both sides, not just a monologue (Tolson and Koenig 2003). Towards the end of life, prayer can help to 'come to an understanding of illness and death and make dying less frightening' (Lo *et al.* 2003, p.410). Prayer can also allow a person to express their hopes and fears and even find solace and acceptance of approaching death (Lo *et al.* 2003).

Fear and anxiety are powerful emotions that can overwhelm us when faced with a crisis and are common to those struggling to find meaning in their dying or bereavement. Having a faith does not prevent a person experiencing fear (Reid 1996); yet, in the face of fear, faith and prayer can provide the strength to go on.

We continue to follow Wendy's story as she cares for her dying husband. Her experience of prayer is described on the following page.

Wendy found that in the times when she was agitated and anxious, often at night, she would turn to prayer. On those nights she found herself getting a sound sleep. The spiritual support that other Christians gave was also invaluable and Wendy felt surrounded by 'love, prayer and care'. She states: 'I felt the Holy Spirit had moved in.'

Another experience of prayer comes from John who cared for his dying wife.[1]

John once asked for something he termed 'palliative prayer' when his wife, Betty, was at the end stage of cancer. Although they desired earthly healing, they recognised that this time it would not come, but they also believed that ultimate healing comes with death and eternal life. They now prayed for peace and comfort, for hope and assurance, placing their trust in God and living each moment until the very last. Many well-meaning friends did not understand this acceptance of death and quite verbally criticised it as a lack of faith. Quite the opposite, it was a crucial act of faith that held them close together in their hour of need.

THE BEST WAY TO PRAY IS YOUR WAY

Prayer is personal and each of us has the right to say how, or even if, we want prayer. Some people are happy knowing that others are praying for them, but don't necessarily want people in the room praying with them. There are also

---

1   John's story is used with his permission.

many written prayers that may provide the comfort that is needed at any given time. Various faiths and cultures have their own ways of praying, and chaplains, or someone from a local church or faith community, are always available to assist. Sometimes people who have never prayed before will turn to prayer in their time of approaching death. Great sensitivity is needed to ensure that the appropriate steps are taken to give the person requesting prayer the comfort he or she is seeking.

HOW DO WE PRAY AS SOMEONE IS DYING?

Should we be praying with them or apart from them? Who should pray, and for what should we pray? Some people feel reluctant to pray in front of others; some don't feel that they have the 'right' words. Whose role is it to pray at these times? To pray with the person or apart from them depends very much on the wishes of the person who is dying. If they have a faith, they will probably want to have others pray with them; even if it seems that they can't participate, just being in the room with the patient is valuable. If the person who is dying does not have a religious faith, then it would be inappropriate to pray in their presence.

It is never appropriate to pray to bring a person to faith, in their presence, if they do not have a religious faith and have not asked for prayer; this is termed proselytising and should not be done. People who are dying are vulnerable and should not be admonished or coerced in the process of their dying.

On the other hand it is appropriate to ask the dying person and his or her family if they would like prayer, or any kind of ritual that may support them in this final journey. In best practice, those who are caring for the dying person will already know what the spiritual and religious beliefs and values of the person are. Pastoral carers and clergy will already be aware of the spiritual and religious needs of the person.

DO WE PRAY FOR HEALING, EVEN WHEN THE PERSON IS DYING?

Christians believe that even in death there is healing. Healing is seen differently from cure. To cure is to remove all signs of disease from the body. Healing is to come to wholeness of being, and this can occur in the presence of disease, as the person grows into wholeness of body, mind and spirit. Healing can come through death, when cure of the physical body is no longer possible. So, it is always appropriate to pray for healing and wholeness.

There is mystery in the process of dying, in that we do not always understand what is happening. Medical staff can provide the best possible prognosis, and the person may die sooner or survive for much longer than has been predicted; it is very difficult to tell how long a person still has to live. Factors that influence dying are complex and include the disease process and the physical resistance of the person, as well as their mental outlook and sense of spiritual hope; that is resilience. Understood in this way, it makes good sense to continue to pray for healing of body, mind and spirit; for hope and peace; and for strength and wholeness.

The person who is dying may be prayed for, and their loved ones too will continue to need strength, endurance, patience, love and peace and hope, which can be requested through prayer.

You can choose if you want to pray and how you want to pray. There is no 'right' or 'wrong' way to pray.

7

Responding to Meaning

Symbol and Ritual

When someone we love is dying

How do we express our sorrow? How do we express our anguish? How can we show what we feel at the very depths of our being? Words often seem superfluous or meaningless. How do we find the right words? Are there really any 'right' words?

Some life experiences touch us so deeply that no words can express our emotion. But often symbol and ritual can do what words cannot. We respond to symbols and rituals if they are meaningful for us. Symbols and rituals, at best, carry meaning. We may remember instances in our communities and in national disasters where rituals have been used effectively to help people to come to terms with a tragedy. Such rituals have included memorial services after bushfires or earthquakes, or after the deaths of numbers of people such as in the Bali bombings, and the September 11 tragedy. In these instances whole communities or nations have mourned, and needed ritual and symbols to connect with the meaning and be carriers of hope, emerging from the grief.

What can we use as symbols? Symbols can be almost anything. A flower, a cross, a candle, a shell, a stone, a tree, a piece of burnt or gnarled wood, gum leaves, autumn leaves, spring flowers, liturgical colours of purple or red, or incense – the list is endless, limited only by imagination. However, not every one of the articles listed would be meaningful to everyone, so it is important to find symbols that carry meaning for ourselves and those we love. Imagination is important here, to be able to see connections with the symbols.

USE OF SYMBOLS

Symbols can carry our stories. A beautiful story has been told of a dying New Zealand woman and the gift of a feather to her by her younger sister (Gregory and Gregory 2004). The younger sister brought the feather with her as she came on a long journey to say goodbye to her older sister. She gave it to her as a symbol of journey. A short time later, as she was dying, the older woman asked for the feather and held it as she died. This was deeply symbolic for the sisters and those gathered around. It was about connections, about journey, about the sacredness of this time.

The crucial factor in choosing which symbols to use is that they are meaningful to the person dying. Kerrie Hide (2002) writes of symbols being 'potent and dynamic', and acting as 'catalysts that invite participation in a fullness that is beyond words and images' (p.85).

Gabrielle wrote of symbols that helped her after her brain surgery and began facing the final months of her life:

- The brown bear symbolizing me, standing hungry, waiting for the right salmon to swim upwards (people). Some you take to fill your hunger for life; others you need to let go by, as Daniel O'Leary says, 'God will take care of the others.'

- The platypus, which was right outside my unit the afternoon I went to hospital. Graceful and contemplative.

The image of a platypus became an important symbol and an anchor for Gabrielle. She had lived close to a river and sometimes saw the platypus there by the riverbank. It was quite amazing that she had seen it that afternoon, as normally these are very shy creatures, and this was a busy part of the river, during the daytime. Later, as her care became palliative, she kept a toy platypus with her. She would hold it and stroke it when she could no longer speak. This platypus seemed to give her comfort in times that were hard. Later, this platypus was placed, with a number of other symbols of her life, on her coffin, during the funeral service.

Another symbol is used in the following story, of a wooden cross that became an important symbol for a family in their experiences faith, life, and grieving.[1]

It was just a little wooden cross that was made from the floorboards of the old church. The hands that so lovingly made the cross knew the Father's heart. The cross was given to Mum some months before she died. She kept it on the table beside her bed where she could see it.

---

1   Story used with permission.

I believe the cross was a reminder of the Father's love for her. It was a symbol of her assurance of salvation. It reminded her that nothing could separate her from His love.

After she died in October 2006 I took the cross home. It sat on the dresser in our spare bedroom. It reminded me of answered prayers. It reminded me of how Jesus had ministered his love to Mum through friends, family and the presence of his Holy Spirit in her room.

Last year Mum's older brother Arthur had to go into a nursing home due to ill health. In March this year we were invited to his 98th birthday party. What gift do you give to someone who is 98? I prayed that I would be able to find a gift that would be meaningful and would bring him hope. I thought of the little wooden cross. I explained to him where it had come from and that I thought Mum would want him to have it.

I didn't see him again after his party. He died a few weeks later. When I spoke to his daughter at the funeral she told me that he had kept that little cross on the table beside his bed where he could see it. She said it had brought him peace. That is just what Jesus said he would bring us. I think for Uncle Arthur the cross reminded him that Jesus died for him and there is nothing that can separate us from God's love.

My cousin asked if I would like to have the cross back but I sensed that she should keep it for now.

Who knows where God will use it next.

WHOSE RITUAL? WHOSE SYMBOLS?

Another question is, whose symbol and whose ritual are these? It might be that loved ones need different rituals than the person who is dying. Choices need to be made carefully. It could be that some ritual that the family would find strengthening, would not be what the dying person would want. Decisions need to be made along the way as to the best rituals for different people. Both the dying person and the family can be helped by means of the right symbols and rituals. This is also important after death, when the focus moves to support those who are grieving.

RITUALS

Symbols can also be used in ritual. What are rituals? A ritual is an ordered way of connecting with meaning, and it often includes the use of symbols. There are formal rituals of the church, but sometimes we need even more rituals in addition to the traditional last rites, anointing, funerals and memorial services. An important part of meeting the needs for connection with loved ones is to make a sacred space. What do we mean by this? A sacred space is somewhere that feels safe, where the people involved can connect with the deepest thoughts and emotions. For people of religious faith, this will be a place where God is present. A sacred space may be a religious place such as a church, temple or mosque; or it can be a space in a garden, in the family home, or in a dying person's room. With care, we can create our sacred spaces.

Rituals can be framed with prayer, poems, and/ or liturgy. Music and art can be valuable in setting the scene for the ritual, and, indeed, can be integral to its effectiveness. It is important for the ritual to be meaningful for the people it is to serve. The best rituals used around dying are often those that engage all who are part of the grief. A ritual that works for people connects them with meaning; it provides a way into difficult topics, like saying final goodbyes, asking and giving forgiveness. Ritual provides a bridge for healing and hope. One article written by authors working in hospice care is titled: 'When there is nothing left to do, there is everything left to do' (Running, Girard and Woodward Tolle 2008). This article tells of the many things that are possible when palliation takes the front running, and when cure can no longer be the goal; it is then that so many things can be done to support and enrich the final times of those who are making this final journey and the journey with their loved ones.

Religious rituals may be very important for some people. People should be encouraged to feel free to engage in these rituals according to their belief systems. It is important that rituals are appropriate to the religious faith of those who are dying, so a basic knowledge of the main dying and death customs of the different major faith groups is important for those working with people who are dying (MacKinlay 2010). The last rites are important for Roman Catholics, and Anglicans and other Christian denominations have specific liturgies and prayers, including confession and pronouncement of absolution of sins, and the offering of Holy Communion for those who are in the last stages of life. There may be great comfort and support for the bereaved in the funeral service, rituals and symbols. For instance, Orthodox Christian communities recognise the importance of continuing rituals and prayers in the grieving process. Often the offering of food within a faith community or within a local secular community can be a great support to those grieving.

How do we find what will be meaningful for a person?

Meaningful experiences

We are all 'meaning makers'; we see life and its meaning through our life experiences and, most importantly, through story. Knowing the person who is dying is such an important starting point, and the way to knowing is to allow – in fact, stronger than that – to encourage the person to speak their story. This story is unique and tied to their identity. It is this story that will form the basis of knowing them and their beliefs, their practices and the ways that they might respond to people, to music, to the arts, to religion, to the environment and creation.

Sacred space

Ritual and symbol can be supported by creating a sacred space. A sacred space is a place that is special, set apart for the deeper things of life. Almost any place can become sacred, with the support of the people involved. A room at home, or in a hospice, can become sacred. How can this be done? Simply clearing away clutter, perhaps bringing flowers, a candle, a cross or other religious article as appropriate for the people present. Many other things can be added – incense, photos or pictures, a bowl of water, oil for anointing. In this way, an ordinary space can be transformed into sacred space.

Silence may be the most appropriate way of being at times. It is important to be aware of the personality of the person who is dying. Did they like singing and talking a lot, or did they like to be quiet? What kind of use of symbols and ritual might speak best to them? The examples below illustrate very different ways of using rituals and symbols, to meet the different needs of different people.

SAYING GOODBYE THROUGH RITUAL AND SYMBOL

Saying goodbye to loved ones is part of the process of dying and can be very hard to do. One way of doing this is through the use of ritual and symbol. Alan Niven (2008) wrote a case study of two rings, where Betty, an 89-year-old widow, knew she was dying and wanted to be able to speak openly to her two daughters – one who accepted the reality of her mother's dying, and the other who seemed unable to accept what lay ahead.

One daughter is very realistic and asks for information but the other does not really want to face the facts and keeps insisting that Mum will one day go home. For Betty, each day becomes a difficult journey of adjusting to the two perspectives of her daughters. Her honest talks with her doctor have revealed to her what she suspected. She is failing rapidly and her doctor is talking in terms of months. One daughter refuses to acknowledge this and the other, who accepts the situation and talks to her mother about it, is becoming more frustrated as the days go by. (Niven 2008, p.224)

Betty felt that giving her rings to her daughters might help, but how was she to do this in these circumstances? Betty had a firm faith, but her daughters did not, although they respected the faith of their mother. The chaplain talked with Betty and together they worked out a simple ritual and prayers, during which the mother could give the rings to her daughters, and all three were guided and supported by the chaplain. This provided the opportunity for the daughter who did not accept the reality of approaching death to come to this new realisation, and for each of them to say goodbye, encompassed by meaningful ritual.

'LET'S HAVE A PARTY'

A woman was dying and 'on the Wednesday Mum said to me she wanted a party. At first I didn't take too much notice of it. Our mum loved her parties and I did not think she was really well enough to cope with a party...' (Bourgeois and Johnson 2004, pp.100–101). The party happened, with her medications timed so that she would be on her best form for the party. Her friends and family came with guitar and songs. This example was fitting for the everyday lifestyle of this woman, who, as she was dying, wanted one more party – this time to say goodbye to those she loved and allow them to say goodbye to her.

What is the meaningful activity that you might want to have, or to do?

8

TRANSCENDENCE IN THE PROCESS OF DEATH AND DYING

HUMOUR AND DYING

Jenny Thompson-Richards is a social worker and a clown who works at Daw House palliative care unit in South Australia. She says: 'We find joy in the midst of suffering' (Thompson-Richards 2006, p.137). Sometimes dying can be pretty grim and it is hard to find anything to laugh about, and yet, at times, humour and joy come and give great relief and a sense of being together on this journey. Jenny describes the clown's tasks as seeking 'to affirm people as people with richly storied lives' (p.139). Part of the process is to connect with the stories of the ones who are dying. This process is an important one for families, too. Have you ever realised, too late, that an aunt, or even your mother or father, had rich stories to tell, and that these had not been shared? The clowns have a way of entering into the stories in a wonderful way.

We can't all be clowns, but we can be present to those close to us during their dying and allow them to share of their stories. I remember well an uncle of mine, about a week before he died, reminiscing about the time that he was on a ship in Darwin Harbour when it was being bombed during World War II. Now, he had little breath, and we crowded around him to listen; we waited for him as he gathered the strength for the next few words. But he laughed as he recounted the story of himself, a radio officer, who knew almost nothing about navigation, being ordered to get the ship away from the dock immediately.

Humour has a special place in the process of both living and dying. Humour can help us through the darkest places, and give us courage for the next steps. Too often we feel that we must be serious in this process of dying. There may be times when humour is right! At these times, let it flow. Sometimes laughter and tears come together. Great sensitivity is needed to match the mood of the person. Connecting with people is so important. One study of humour and dying (Dean and Major 2008) concludes that humour is a way of affirming connections between the dying person, their carers and staff.

One of the things about being on a journey towards death, is that a degree of transcendence may occur; when it does, there are deep and special experiences for the person and their families. The person who is dying may seem to move beyond the distress and pain to, apparently, another plane; perhaps a place of peace that others may find hard to reach.

Dark humour may be used by the person who is dying, in the very face of death. Sometimes that makes it easier for the person to cope; it puts a distance between them and whatever they are facing at the time. One elderly woman, whose friend, living alone, had been found about a week after her death, remarked as she considered her own death: 'Well, I guess the cats would eat me';[1] she had several cats and worried about who would feed them if she died alone.

---

[1]   Transcript of interview for doctoral studies (MacKinlay 1996).

Humour needs to be used both spontaneously and sensitively so as to maintain and affirm the dignity of the dying person. Humour is very individual and cannot be forced; and sometimes humour is just not appropriate, so it is important to be guided by the person themselves. Different cultures of the person and the carer may mean that humour could be misunderstood in some cases. One study of the use of humour in hospice settings (Adamle and Ludwick 2005) found that humour was used in 85 percent of observed nurse visits, and that 70 percent of these were initiated by the dying person, underlining the importance of the interaction with the person who is dying.

FACING LIFE IN THE MIDST OF TREATMENTS: POSSIBILITIES FOR TRANSCENDENCE

Gabrielle faced radiotherapy and chemotherapy for a brain tumour before her care became palliative. She wrote of coming to terms with her life and the way ahead.[2] There are signs of transcendence in her reflections, written during the final two weeks of radiotherapy.

---

2   Gabrielle's condition was diagnosed July 2009. She was at that time working at the Centre for Ageing and Pastoral Studies, in Canberra where she brought her love of people and her passion for caring for those with dementia to inform her vocation. Her own journey towards death was marked with the loss of speech and stroke that made her very dependent, and she well knew what lay before her and journeyed this road with a graciousness informed by her faith. Her words may be helpful to others who face this journey themselves, or for their loved ones. Gabrielle Brian died on 22 October 2010 and in the last months of her illness lost the ability to speak, but not her smile. She was an inspiration to all who cared for her during this time.

Yesterday was a turning point, I think. I was feeling despondent about my physical losses – memory especially – and writing – although that has been worse – and counting. Then it turned around – to enjoy my remaining skills, as in the care of people with dementia. I no longer felt like a little battered lady, but someone facing a golden adventure – like when I bought my house and I saw it as an adventure. The *work* I need to do.

Ernest Hemingway: 'Life breaks everybody, and some people grow at the broken places.'

Mel Kimble: 'I have discovered that my basic faith in an Ultimate Being who has brought me to the present can be trusted as I face the uncertain and shadowy future.' Wow!

I am aware of the vulnerabilities being highlighted due to the medication – it's good to be aware of it.

Somehow I find it easier to make the experience a prayer for a particular person, perhaps going through radiography, like the indigenous lady who has breast cancer and a brain tumour. I am also aware of keeping my world 'big'. It suits me as well to reach out to others. How do we pray 'when our experiences become the raw material of our prayer'? I've read about cancer and the benefits of meditation. Each time I try to meditate I fall asleep straight away or am distracted. This is reassuring – my experience *is* a prayer.

Albert Camus: 'In the midst of winter I finally learned that there was in me an invincible summer.'

Today it dawned on me – 'God is Love!' All the love and care I'm receiving, that is God.

9

Healing of Relationships

One of the opportunities in the process of dying may be the opportunity to review one's life and to come to a sense of reconciliation with those we love and perhaps have been separated from over the years. Issues over incidents that happened perhaps many years ago may still colour our lives, and anger, bitterness, resentment may prevent us coming to a sense of hope and peace as we face death, whether it be our own, or the death of someone we love. We don't always realise the things we need to change or to deal with, until a crisis hits.

The following story illustrates some of these issues.

Edith[1] (76 years) describes her change of attitude after recovering from a cardiac arrest. She said that 'she thought she was back to all her miseries again, it took her a while to adjust to being back (alive).' She explained how she regretted being brought back to life, that everything in her life seemed to be wrong.

I was rowing with my daughter, I was rowing with my son. They couldn't understand, it just seemed

---

1   Not her real name: identities of all people protected, unless permission has been given that the person has clearly indicated that they wish to have their real name used. Permission has been given for all material used in this publication.

I [was] going back years, blaming myself for my husband's death and everything just, caught up. And I hated people. And that was one of the things in my life that was very wrong... And when I had the cardiac arrest, and then when I had the bypass, the bypass mainly, I found I was looking at things differently... I wasn't angry anymore. And other things that had been upsetting me, I thought I was looking at them with an entirely different opinion. But I was looking at it and I wasn't condemning like I did... I feel that the purpose was I was going out hating, and I shouldn't be allowed to go out [that is, to die] hating. And I'd been brought back to show the reason for it and why I still have a purpose in life, even if it's only a short one. (MacKinlay 2001, p.173)

Edith asked an important question, 'Why was I brought back?' Her response to her question was important in her search. This resulted in finding a new purpose and meaning in life. As Edith reflected on her journey, both before and after her arrest, she was moved to write a poem on fear. The poem illustrates some of the difficulties she has struggled with over the last years, and the working through and changing of her attitudes.

'Tis fear that I'm really afraid of,
that I'll not be able to conceal it
and I'll show my shame to all
I would like to live a little longer,
to see my grandsons grow taller
please Lord, grant me courage to face it well
let me laugh when I feel like screaming loud
let me think of those who gave a helping hand
and let me cast out the anger I had
at those who hurt me through the pages of my life
anger, fears, and contempt

why did I let these thoughts twist my mind?
they only destroy the good within us all
we can change these thoughts
for God is still there within our soul.

(MacKinlay 2001, pp.173–174)

Following her cardiac arrest, Edith is aware of her struggle to overcome hate and anger in her life, and she shows that older people can and do change. She is able to manage well in the face of uncertainty, to let go of issues. In recent times she has returned to her faith, and this has also provided comfort for her.

GUILT AND DYING

It is possible to carry guilt for some action, or omission of action, for many years, without arriving at any resolution of that guilt. Often the guilt lies deeply buried and it is only when the person is approaching death that the issue becomes prominent and in need of resolution and healing. Confession begins the process of healing the guilt.

CONFESSION, FORGIVENESS AND RECONCILIATION

Guilt, anger and hatred can overwhelm and prevent us from growing spiritually and can prevent healing. Reconciliation, forgiveness and confession are important parts of living, of spiritual growth and well-being. They are parts of being human that we need to get right before we come to the ends of our lives. Which comes first? In fact we can't be reconciled with anyone unless we are first able to let go of the hurt and pain, the feeling of being 'wronged'. Sometimes that also involves recognising that we have hurt someone too. That is hard to do. But it is only if we are able to let go of our pain and hurt that we can be healed of that. (This is sometimes called 'existential' pain; see Chapter 5.) So this means, first, confession, even to ourselves, that we have done something that has hurt another person. Second, it means that we need to forgive and to be forgiven, and to come third, to a point of reconciliation. The desire for revenge or retaliation leads to estrangement, not healing.

Put simply, the sequence is:

1. admitting that we could have been wrong in what we did, or failed to do (confession)
2. letting go of the event, letting go of the hurt or feelings of anger against another (forgiveness)
3. a new start (reconciliation).

CONFESSION

Sometimes the need for confession starts to come from a growing sense of discomfort or guilt, sometimes from resentment over some action of another person towards us, or a sense that we ourselves have wronged someone. This may be seen in a religious perspective or in a secular context. It is as we begin to reminisce that we find these bits of unfinished business that may prevent us from finding peace. Some things from our past just need to be let go of. Some things are quite challenging and more difficult to deal with.

One frail elderly woman, Violet, was estranged from her son and had major problems with her daughter-in-law. The situation could not be dealt with fully at that time, as, although the mother longed to be at peace with her son and daughter-in-law, they remained estranged. Perhaps a time would come when they could be reconciled, but in the meantime, what could help Violet? Violet was able to go back over her life and let go of the resentments and anger she felt towards her daughter-in-law, whom she blamed for the broken relationship between herself and her son.

This meant that Violet had, first, to recognise her need to let go of these emotions so that she could find peace. This could mean just recognising any part she had played in the estrangement, admitting to herself if she had been at fault. In some cases, it may need to be talked through with a trusted friend. In some cases of deep-seated resentment, and perhaps even hate, counselling, or confession of thoughts and deeds may be needed. For Christians of some denominations, confession to a priest may be required, and that may have healing effects as the person – Violet, in this case – is able to let go of the thing that was binding her. New life can come from this. Confession can come, even when there is no way in which the person can meet with or be reconciled with the other. In this case, forgiveness by the other person will not be experienced; however, forgiveness by God, for those who believe, will bring real healing.

FORGIVENESS

Forgiveness can be seen in religious or non-religious terms. There are clear guidelines in Christian Scripture supporting the importance of forgiveness. In case forgiving is seen simply as a religious action, a secular definition is offered here, by Pingleton in Festa and Tuck (2000), saying that 'forgiveness is the voluntary letting go of the right to retaliate after injury' (p.79). Forgiveness may also be seen as giving up deeply held values and replacing them with new ones (Pargament 1997). Forgiveness brings freedom and peace. Where this happens, it is one of the joys that sometimes comes during the final stage of a person's life. Sometimes knowing that death is imminent brings people to a new place, being willing to admit guilt and wrongdoing and asking forgiveness. This is, after all, the last opportunity that a person has to put things 'right'.

TABLE 9.1 A PROCESS OF FORGIVENESS[2]

I won't forgive.	Still holds the hurt.
I can't forgive.	Feels unable to move to forgive.
Should I forgive?	Begins to ask, 'Perhaps I can forgive – maybe I need to forgive?'
Process of forgiving.	Acknowledges the need to forgive and enters into the process.

RECONCILIATION: A CHANCE TO SAY GOODBYE, A CHANCE TO SAY 'SORRY'

How can we be reconciled with those from whom we have grown apart? My uncle was dying, and my mother, who had advanced dementia, lived in another city. We adult children realised that they had not always been

---

2   Table based on Mickley and Cowles (2001).

close. My sister wasn't sure that Mum would know what she was talking about, but she told Mum about her brother. They both responded to each other and each sent flowers and a note to the other. There was a good feeling in the family about that, and I am sure that for both my mother and my uncle, there was at least some healing.

It is not always possible to see someone face-to-face and be reconciled. Sometimes the other person does not want to meet, or they may have died without the opportunity for healing and closure. But it is still possible to make some act of reaching out to the other person. Anger and hatred are powerful feelings that may go deep into the person and cause much anguish. Of course, reconciliation is not possible without forgiveness.

10

INTIMACY AND DYING

Significant losses can be of partner, parent, child and friend; I have already outlined issues of grief and loss in Chapter 1. The nature of the relationship is reflected in the intensity of the grief.

The importance of relationship is highlighted by Deck and Folta (in De Vries 2001), who wrote that a study of grief 'is the study of people and their most intimate relationships' (p.75). It is sometimes only in grief that the true significance of the relationship can be realised.

> • Intimacy is a deep and spiritual human need.
> • 'At the deepest core of my being, I need to be known and loved as I am.'
>
> (Carroll and Dyckman 1986, p.123)

Sexual relationships may still be important for some in this final journey, but for many, features of the process of dying make this difficult. However, intimacy is about far more than sexual performance. Intimacy is at best the sense of being known and loved at the depths of one's being. Dying and death can strengthen and also test the bonds of relationship.

Even though the pain relief drugs made it difficult for Lewis to remember things, at other times we had very good communication. Keeping Lewis comfortable and at home worked. Looking after myself, as the carer, also worked. Yet while I had a firm acceptance of the situation, it didn't take much to unsettle me. Lewis maintained his sense of humour, and although we didn't do as much as in the past, we continued to grab the opportunities as they arose. As I say, not every person has the chance to sleep with his nurse. We would tell each other how we felt regularly, our ups and downs, or just our tiredness, what was comfortable or what was not comfortable. My commitment to Lewis's needs continued to reassure him, as well as our love. Medical people expressed their care by loading us up with additional medical supplies and equipment. Caring support came unexpectedly from many, some of whom we didn't know very well. Our team of minders continued to support us even though it was a long journey. They all knew Lewis well and played an important role in keeping both of us focused each day. For Lewis it was social interaction with visitors, while for me it was going for a walk with the neighbour's dog. Our home continued to be a place of peace as we all learnt that this final journey can be gentle and loving, and not one to be feared.

After the death of a loved one, it is not uncommon to continue to want to talk with them. For example, one widow said: '...I couldn't foresee how awkward life would be when I couldn't look across the kitchen table and ask, 'Is "tenant" spelt "ent" or "ant"?' (Jones in De Vries 2001, p.76).

In fact, it is not uncommon for bereaved people to talk to their loved one who has died. One elderly widow told me that she often checked, before making a decision, by speaking to her late husband's photo: she would think and ask, 'What would you have done [in this or that situation]?' So it can be correctly stated that 'death marks the end of a life, not the end of a relationship' (Deck and Folta 1989, p.76). It is not wrong to keep the relationship – not as an obsessive focus on the deceased person, but as engagement in an ongoing, albeit changed, bond of intimacy. In fact this bond, may give the bereaved person strength in the face of enormous loss.

SIGNIFICANT PEOPLE WHO CARE

Sometimes there are few family members near. Others may then become 'significant people' to the person who is dying. Gabrielle wrote of those who supported her in the process of treatment in the hospital.

Other people – never have I known so many generous, loving people, including the staff at Canberra hospital, so filled with kindness and goodness.

People who have made a difference – I discovered the importance of the mixture of compassionate and medical care. It is the compassion that I remember most, e.g. I remember the spiritual aspects of a conversation with a nurse in recovery, even though it wouldn't be expected that I would remember it following the operation, and another nurse with his kindness. Yet another nurse invited me to think of Joan of Arc and that really touched me, thereby inviting me to a spiritual conversation. I was touched by yet another making me a jam sandwich at 2.00am in the morning.

DYING AND BEING WITH FRIENDS

Intimacies in later life are still important, but for frail older people close relationships are more likely to become fragile and uncertain. Win told of her friend who was very frail, and she described the last time they spent together.

I'd had the thought to go over and see her that afternoon, and oh I thought, oh dear it's too hot, don't know whether I'll bother, and then I thought, no I will (go and visit her) I'm halfway there. I'll go up and see her. And so we had a wonderful talk about death and dying and she said 'I don't think I'll see my 95th birthday' or something like that, she said and I could tell she was [Win paused]. She said her legs were aching so I said 'Well shall I rub your legs?' so I rubbed her legs and the next day I heard that she'd died, and I thought well you know, obey, obeying the whisper of guidance really was the thing that you know. I felt sad that she had died but I felt so grateful that I'd had that time with her before she died. (MacKinlay 2001, p.213)

It seemed natural that these two friends should talk about death, on that last day before one of them died. Win spoke of a 'whisper of guidance'[1] that had urged her to visit. It seems there was a deep connecting, perhaps a sharing of sacred space between these two women during that visit. The next day Win heard that her friend had died; she expressed both a sense of loss and also gratitude for her visit the day before. Win had a deep sense of spirituality and abundant spiritual strategies sustained through close relationship with her God, and she continued in study,

---

1   In the tape recording it was obvious that Win regarded the source of guidance as the Holy Spirit.

prayer and Christian meditation. This enabled Win to be open to spiritual matters and to be present to others in the deeper issues of life (MacKinlay 2001, p.213).

TAKING ON THE ROLE OF CARER

This can be an emotionally draining time for all those who are close to the person who is dying. Often, before acceptance comes struggle, and in this struggle there will be the daily working through of care needs, which will change over time and will need continuing reassessment. Uncertainty, and simply putting one foot in front of the other, become ways of life. Wendy has wise words based on her journey in the role of carer.

Being a carer for your husband is not an easy role as you go through the grieving stages, like him, and in my case, at different times. To try and be positive when with him and then be in tears while being by yourself is a lonely journey. I became aware of the medical problems and requested answers long before Lewis realised he was so ill. Understandably the specialists didn't want to give us a time frame of what to expect but fortunately our GP, who is also a friend and a Christian, understood my need to know even though Lewis preferred to stay unaware – or maybe not. If I knew what to expect, I could manage most times. The minefield of paperwork, systems, supplies, medicines and knowledge of nursing was a challenge and I continually wondered how others coped. I was 21 years younger than Lewis and reasonably fit, with a good education, as well as being trained in first aid. The hardest thing was to tell others the prognosis for the first time. The non-breathing times of sleep apnoea were stressful as well as waking up in the morning and wondering if Lewis was still alive. We slept in our queen-size bed together at night. I began to acquire a lot of knowledge about caring for a sick person. The palliative care nurse said I have completed about half of the nurses' training.

As a carer, and for a coping mechanism, I stopped family or other visitors staying overnight during this period. Lewis tired very easily and I did not have the extra energy to look after others. We had some nights with disturbed sleep and coping with visitors became an intrusion.

BURDENS AND JOYS

Being a carer can be both a burden and a joy. Until recently, much of the research focused on the burden of caring, and there certainly is an element of burden in care; however, that is only part of the picture and now more research has been done that asked different questions, not assuming that all care was burden. The results were surprising to some. One article focused on the experience of caring for people with dementia in the terminal stages (Netto, Goh and Yap 2009). The questions asked allowed the carers to tell of the joys and benefits to them of caring, as well as the hard parts.

Henry Nouwen (1994) writes that 'to care is the privilege of every person and is at the heart of being human' (p.66). He also suggests that we need to befriend our own death so we can help others to befriend theirs. 'Every step we take toward a deeper self-understanding [of death], is also a step that brings us closer to those with whom we share our lives' (p.65).

In caring for the dying, we need to be able to sit beside them as they journey, hold their hand, listen to their stories and their fears, and be open to their spiritual needs, as well as attending to their physical comforts. There are times when the burden of caring becomes overwhelming and a sense of helplessness may creep up on you. It is good to acknowledge that the carer cannot do it alone. Friends, family, support groups, faith groups, all play an important part in caring for the carer.

There are also treasured times of profound joy that may almost seem inappropriate yet can become the sustaining essence of caring for our loved ones. In his book *A Funny Thing Happened on the Way to the Nursing Home* Jim Connor (1997) talks of the privilege of caring for his wife, Norma, at home until she died. Jim explains that he was fortunate to have his own good health and to be surrounded by a circle of love from family and friends. He reflects that none of us are perfect and that we will all fall at some stage, but he also believes that 'laughter is the best medicine, and if carers can learn to laugh with one another over incidents that others would see as tragic, then we might just be able to help one another up after we fall' (p.vi).

PRESERVING THE DOMESTIC REALM

It is not always easy to know how to respond to the needs of others to 'do good'. Some offers of help are invaluable, and part of this final journey is surely about learning how to accept offers of help that will support both the carer and the person who is dying. It is also important to learn how to say 'no' to offers of help that are not seen to be in the interests of the person who is dying and their primary carer. Wendy's experience illustrates the wisdom of this.

I had many offers of help from family, our church family and friends. During this period I felt the need to take up many of these offers. However, I did have doubts about the motives of a few people. These offers I politely did not take up. Lewis could not be left for periods longer than two hours so it was arranged for various visitors (minders) to drop in, make a cuppa for all and stay for a short visit. This enabled me to take time out for my music, walks, swims, lunch with friends, a film, Indonesian session, or my fortnightly massage, and prevented any feelings of regret at putting my life on hold. I also realised that I was not eating properly, nor did I have a routine. I addressed this and structured my day with regular meal breaks and a properly prepared diet. When I reached the stage that I didn't want to get out of bed in the mornings, I knew that I had to look after myself as well as Lewis. For us it was a long journey. My energy levels did increase as well as my sense of purpose and motivation for each day. I was able to cope with less emotion when things didn't go as planned and just tried to rectify the situation.

The carer at home has the advantage of being on home territory and any who come into the home to give care come as guests. The person dying is in a familiar environment and a sense of normality can be maintained to a large extent, even when treatments and disability aids are in evidence, such as walking frames, shower chairs, etc.

Wendy also spoke of the need to take time out.

For me as a carer time out each day was beneficial in three aspects. Lewis would have a much valued social interaction as the visitor became part of the journey. He was a great listener and enjoyed being with others.

This probably dispelled many of the myths the visitor (minder) had of dying as well as being able to do something for a person they cared for and loved. For me as the carer, it was often a time of physical activity, crying and prayer. As I walked through the bush tracks I could still appreciate the beauty of God's world, the mountains, trees and animals. Was it easy to leave Lewis even for such a short time? No. But our palliative nurse, Salli, said she wishes other carers would do this and reaffirmed my daily time out. This was an important aspect of being able to sustain being a carer for 20 months and coping with eventually seven more medical problems as they surfaced.

Respite for a carer, whether short or long term, is not only OK, but necessary emotionally, physically and cognitively.

CARER AS A VISITOR IN THE HOSPICE OR AGED CARE FACILITY: HOW TO MAKE IT LIKE HOME

On the other hand, when the person who is dying is in an aged care facility or hospice, there are naturally many more restrictions on movements of the resident and family. The challenge is to make the institution as much like home as possible. Many hospices do provide welcoming environments without the clinical signs of a hospital. Getting to know the staff and working with them to make the environment as comfortable as possible is important, as they will be able to suggest ways to personalise the person's room. It may help to bring in things that are important to the person who is dying, for example, photos, a favourite ornament, and other articles that are reminders of home.

BEING A COMPANION ALONG THE WAY

Caring for a person who is dying can be a special time of intimacy. The relationship between loved ones can change through the experience of caring. Some experience the caring role as a burden, while others find that caring, although extremely challenging and tiring, may be a time of personal spiritual growth and even a time of enriching the relationship. Even so, the caregiver may need support of others, to be able to share the caring and to have time out to be refreshed. The caring relationship may be complex; the person who is dying may even be the one caring for the carer. The person dying may need to journey with the carer through the carer's grief, while the carer journeys with the person dying through theirs. It may be hard for carers not sharing their grief with those they are caring for. The person dying obviously already has a lot to deal with in their own journey towards death, but although he or she may still want to be that friend and support, that opportunity may not be given (or it may not be possible emotionally to be that friend).

So often loved ones feel helpless as they wait; we have been conditioned to think that we are only helping if we are doing something. Simply sitting and being with the person who is dying may feel uncomfortable. We have been trained that way by many life experiences. In this final life journey, often 'doing' is 'being'. Words may not be necessary. On the other hand, the person who is dying may really want to talk. They may have little energy and tire quickly.

We use the term 'spirituality' on this final journey. Spirituality in palliative care and dying is about accompanying someone on the last significant journey of their lives. It's about intimacy; it's about sharing; and it's about listening, even when the person may not seem to be able to speak. The listening is done with all your senses, not just ears.

11

DEMENTIA AND DYING

Dementia is the overall term used to describe the condition typified by progressive loss of memory and other cognitive functions. The most common and well-known dementia is Alzheimer's Disease; the next most common dementia is vascular dementia;[1] fronto-temporal dementia and several other types of dementia are less commonly occurring types of dementia. Dementia types are described in a number of books and resources (including Alzheimer's Australia 2005; Cayton, Graham and Warner 2004). Dementia is a progressive disease, and communication becomes increasingly difficult for many of these people. At some point, the person with dementia will come to the stage of needing palliative care.

Dementia is feared by many; some people still believe that the person 'dies twice' as their loved one is lost to them, first as they become a 'non-person', and then later as they physically die. Commonly held views about dementia assume that the person with dementia is unaware of, and unable to communicate with, others. Recent research has shown that the person remains, and that in this disease the person is typically seen with loss of memory and often other behaviour changes, and struggles to communicate effectively with others. Words may be lost, but in newer understandings of dementia the person is still there. They

---

1   Vascular dementia is a term which is applied to dementia arising from small strokes.

do not lose the 'self'; it is communicating with others that becomes so difficult (see Hughes, Louw and Sabat 2006; Killick 2004; Killick and Allan 2001; Kitwood 1997; Goldsmith 1996; McFadden and Hanusa 1998; MacKinlay 2006).

A number of authors now challenge the older view of dementia and describe numerous instances where a person with dementia demonstrates considerable communication skill and insight, if only carers are willing to take the time to listen and use alternative communication strategies.

> In dementia: the *person* is still there.

Ways of effectively communicating with people who have moderate to higher levels of dementia have been demonstrated by MacKinlay *et al.* (2010).[2] For instance, spiritual reminiscence using techniques designed for use with people with dementia (MacKinlay 2006) have been found to be effective in connecting with them. The assumption underlying these techniques is that the person remains, but is experiencing problems with communicating.

Strategies used to communicate effectively with people who have moderate to advanced dementia need to focus on connecting with meaning rather than facts. The cognitive difficulties that affect memory and other factual information that the person may need to deal with do

---

2   Research funded by a grant from The J.O. and J.R. Wicking Trust, which is managed by ANZ Trustees. This project trialled programs to reduce levels of depression in people with dementia. An important finding of this study was the significant effect of the facilitator communication style in enabling communication of the people with dementia. It was found that facilitator style was more important than the measured cognitive status of the participants.

not affect his or her ability to respond to emotional and spiritual factors.

Christine Bryden, a person with dementia, wrote: 'Don't abandon me at any stage, for the Holy Spirit connects us. It links our souls, our spirits – not our minds or brains. I need you to minister to me, to be my memory for me' (Bryden and MacKinlay 2002, p.74).

TALKING OF DEATH AMONG PEOPLE WITH DEMENTIA

'Don't tell him, he won't remember anyway.' This is often heard when discussing whether a person with dementia should be told when a family member or friend dies. Yet we have found that in small, facilitated groups people with dementia did talk about the death of one of their group members. This has happened not just in one instance, but in many different settings. On the other hand, where staff did *not* give the opportunity for the topic of death of people known to group members to be raised, then often it was not spoken of.

An example of a member of a small group, who died between one week's session and the next, is given below.[3] When the group next met, the facilitator spoke of the death and enabled the remaining group participants to enter into the grieving process. All the participants in this group had significant dementia. The programme planned for the day was put aside to focus on the immediate needs of the group participants at this time. This served to affirm the group

---

3   An excerpt from the transcripts of the research project: *Minimising the impact of depression and dementia for elders in residential care*. Project was funded by a grant from The J.O. & J.R. Wicking Trust which is managed by ANZ Trustees (2007–2010) MacKinlay, McDonald, Niven *et al.*

members as people of worth and enabled them to enter into the process of grieving. Nearly the whole session was devoted to grief and loss, as the group facilitator gently journeyed with these participants.

Facilitator: We'll look at that, but before we do that I think it would be lovely if we just spent some time thinking of Carrie, who died suddenly late last week, and I understand her...was her funeral yesterday?

Assistant: Mm.

Facilitator: Yesterday?

[Assistant nodding her head.]

Facilitator: Mm. Yes. Very sudden. Very sudden.

Amelia: She didn't. She looked so fit and...

Facilitator: Mm...and maybe we could just think of memories of Carrie, and you might want to share some of those memories.

[The group shared memories about Carrie for at least half an hour.]

Adeline: Yeah.

Facilitator: All right. Let's take a moment in prayer... [The group facilitator gathered together their memories and prayed.]

Adeline: Amen.

The facilitator used prayer appropriately with this small group of people with dementia; she knew already what their background was, and she was leading effective pastoral care.

RITUAL AND PASTORAL CARE FOR PEOPLE WITH DEMENTIA WHO ARE DYING

Ritual is far more important than simply passing the time; it provides an important link into the person. (See Chapter 7, 'Responding to Meaning: Symbol and Ritual'.)

Fay wrote of her husband 'who spent his working life at the core of the caring professions, developed a rare frontal lobe dementia some years ago and ended his days mute and immobile and in need of total care... Eighteen months before his death my husband developed cancer and it was then that regular [pastoral] visitation and communion was re-instated. Communion days saw my husband more alert. He fought to stay awake, following the service with his eyes, and even on occasion took the bread in his hand (a hand that hadn't moved for several years). Any improvement in my husband's condition lifted my spirits also so the ministry was doubly valuable.[4]

Fay was critical of the fact that pastoral care had not been considered important for someone who had dementia, but was seen as important once her husband had been diagnosed with cancer (MacKinlay 2008, pp.46–47).

---

4   Excerpt from a letter written by Fay to Elizabeth MacKinlay, following the death of Fay's husband.

> All people are in need of support in their vulnerability, and the level of cognitive abilities should not make any difference.

There are special ways of communicating with people who have moderate to high level dementia.

> Points to remember when speaking with people who have moderate or more severe dementia:
>
> • Call the person by name when addressing them.
> • Speak slowly and distinctly.
> • Do not patronise or use 'elder speak'.[5]
> • Ask one question at a time.
> • Pause long enough between questions (may need up to five or six seconds between questions).

Do not be afraid to leave a space between sentences. We found that often people with dementia did not respond if the facilitator spoke too quickly. A pause of five or six seconds may seem an uncomfortably long time to some people, but it may be necessary to give the person with dementia time to process what is being asked.

---

5 'Elder speak' is a term used to describe the way older people are sometimes spoken to, using higher tone of voice, speaking loudly and speaking down to the person, as if they would not be able to understand.

CAN PEOPLE WITH DEMENTIA RESPOND TO THE RELIGIOUS AND SPIRITUAL?

Can people who have final stage dementia still respond to the religious and spiritual? There are many instances where they have been able to do so. It seems that their needs may be addressed by making the assumption that they *will* benefit from being engaged in rituals and the use of symbols. Knowing the spiritual and religious background of people with dementia is important; giving relevant and appropriate care is essential for their well-being. Holy Communion, prayer, music and other religious practices according to their faith background are all of great value.

People with dementia can often respond emotionally long after they have difficulty in expressing their thoughts clearly in speech. As Malcolm Goldsmith (2001) reminds us, just about every emotion can be expressed without words: 'love, friendship, fear, jealousy, anticipation puzzlement, anger or hatred' (p.142). Nonverbal communication is also important for people who have dementia. People with dementia can and do respond well to rituals and to the liturgy of a church service. Goldsmith writes of the fact that at least some of ritual is experienced at a subconscious level and does not depend on memory; this is perhaps one of the reasons why ritual remains so important to people who have dementia. An example is given by Oliver Sacks of 'Jimmy': Sacks did not think that Jimmy could respond cognitively to anything, but he did respond to the words of liturgy in the chapel, which was surprising even for this great neurologist (Sacks 1998, pp.23–42). We too often diminish in our own minds what we think a person with dementia can take in or respond to.

KNOWING WHEN THEY ARE DYING?

There are stories of people who are dying who seem to wait until a particular family member arrives, sometimes from a great distance, to say goodbye. This has been observed in some cases for people with dementia too, giving further evidence that the person is still there, even though he or she may not be able to communicate by speech. I well remember travelling a long distance overnight to see my mother when she had dementia and was dying. My daughter and I had 15 minutes with her in which we were able to say goodbye, before she died, very peacefully, in our presence. Although she had not spoken for the previous two years, she was certainly present to us on that last morning; it seemed that she was wide awake, taking in every word we said. It was a very special time – a sacred time, quite brief, but something we will always remember.

12

Ethical and Moral Issues in Dying and Death

There are important ethical and moral issues around dying and quality of life. There are also myths about the process of dying. We hope to provide some guidelines that will be helpful in decision making in these difficult issues and improve quality of life for the older person who is dying.

Preparing for the final journey: Advance Directives and other necessary things

It is hard to think clearly and make the best decisions when there is a sudden change in the person's condition, or when an emergency occurs. 'Advance Directives' are valuable to have in place, even for middle-aged or younger adults. Advance Directives give the person the opportunity to set out their desires for treatment and withholding of treatment in end-of-life decisions, if they are not able to communicate their wishes at that time.

A trusted person, usually a family member, can be appointed with Enduring Power of Attorney (EPA) to follow through on the person's wishes as recorded in the Advance Directive form. Many state bodies now have Advance

Directive forms drawn up, that take legal requirements into account. A copy of the person's document must be made available to those managing medical care. The person holding EPA must also have the documents and inform other family members, as needed, of the wishes of the person dying.

It is helpful for family members to be able to discuss end-of-life issues long before decisions need to be made. However, where this has not been done ahead of time, it should be addressed with the dying person and his or her family with great sensitivity and care. Medical practitioners, social workers and chaplains may be very helpful supporters at this time.

With advance directives and EPA in place everyone is clear about what the expected decisions would be. Wendy and Lewis saw the need for this in time for their planning to be put in place.

We each signed our power of attorney. Lewis's was an Enduring Power of Attorney, that is, if he could not mentally make decisions for himself I could do that for him, not only financially, but medically. This was a sensible step. At one point he had such a high temperature that his brain could not process the information to walk. The palliative care nurse enquired if Lewis had secondaries of the cancer – brain metastasis was mentioned. Imagine that possibility suddenly being presented. Fortunately, it was only a rather nasty infection causing the temperature. Lewis later stayed on antibiotics continuously. At times like that my heart would take a nasty thump.

EUTHANASIA

There is confusion about the term 'euthanasia' and it is important to place this into perspective when considering end-of-life issues. A good definition of euthanasia by bioethicist Dr Megan Best (2010) is 'an act where a doctor intentionally ends the life of a person, by the administration of drugs, at that person's voluntary and competent request, for reasons of compassion' (p.4). Euthanasia is *not* withdrawal of treatment or management of symptoms at the end of life. Euthanasia remains illegal in Australia and in many other countries.

WHEN SHOULD ACTIVE TREATMENT BE DISCONTINUED AND PALLIATIVE CARE BEGIN?

This is one of the most difficult times to be faced, both for the person and for his or her family, on the journey towards death. The right time is not always clear-cut, and different people will have different opinions. Opinions will differ as to whether extra chemotherapy, or other treatments that would perhaps be distressing for the person, ought to be offered and/or carried out. Often families are torn over this decision, some relatives wanting to continue all possible treatments, while others in the same family will want the opposite. Sometimes the opinions of medical practitioners to discontinue treatment may not really be heard, in the hope that there might still be hope of cure, or at least significant improvement. Facing death is always hard. It must always be realised that human life cannot be extended indefinitely.

An important factor that must be considered is whether there is a real hope of improvement in quality of life, or whether further active treatment will cause more burden and distress for the dying person, without real benefit.

TO TREAT OR NOT TO TREAT?

There comes a time when it is not in the best interests of the dying person to continue active treatment, whether this is for cancer or in dementia or other chronic diseases. It is then that life goals change, to bring the focus of care onto quality of remaining life, rather than futile attempts to cure during the process of dying. There is still often reluctance to acknowledge this point. Often, family members do not want to face the beginning of this hard part of the journey, sometimes denying the facts until near to the point of death. It is often the dying person who is more aware of the situation but sometimes cannot speak of it with family members who are not ready to face the loss of their loved one through death. At other times, the person who is dying cannot bear to speak with their loved ones about dying. The decisions are complex.

A distinction needs to be made between:

- treatment to improve the patient's condition, and
- treatment that will prolong the process of dying.

WHEN IS A PERSON ON A DYING TRAJECTORY?

In other words, is there a time when death is inevitable and treatment may increase suffering and prolong the dying process? There usually is, although it can be very hard to see a clear cut-off point, that is, a point when it first becomes obvious that the time has come to say 'no' to active treatment. There comes a stage when it can be futile to intervene to prevent death, and further treatments would only cause distress and suffering for the patient, without any benefits.

The reason why it can be hard to detect when the time is right to cease active treatment is that each case is different and must be carefully considered. There are many facts to be taken into consideration. For instance, an elderly person may have cardiac failure and become delirious. He or she may seem extremely ill, but it may yet be possible, with effective treatment, to recover completely and have good quality of life, even for some years after that event.

On the other hand, a person with end-stage dementia, who has been gradually deteriorating in their overall health over a long period of time, and who can no longer swallow, should not have artificial means of nutrition instituted,[1] but carers continue only to offer drinks and keep the person's mouth moist. The person should be cared for with best quality palliative care that includes care of body, mind and spirit. Inability of the dying person and/or their family to discuss issues around dying openly may be a problem; this factor may be influenced by cultural differences.

---

1   The means which would not be appropriate under these conditions would be PEG (percutaneous endoscopic gastrostomy) tube feeds and nasogastric feeds. PEG tubes can cause a number of serious side effects and be distressing for the patient. Nasogastric tubes are very distressing for the patient. These means of providing nourishment only serve to prolong the process of dying and add to the discomfort of the patient.

TO PROVIDE FOOD AND FLUIDS TO PEOPLE WHO ARE DYING OR NOT?

There is a close link between food and care, and it may be painful to see a loved one losing weight and unable to eat. Frank Brennan (2010) gives an example of a woman who was dying from pancreatic cancer, and had no appetite and was losing weight. Her family were distressed and asked 'She doesn't eat, can't she have a drip to feed her, doctor? ...I've heard of tubes into the stomach' (p.21). However, recent studies have clearly shown that there comes a time when providing food and fluid to a person who is dying is not in their best interests. In fact, 'There is no evidence that medically administered nutrition and hydration improves comfort or dignity during the dying process and, further, Ashby and Mendelson make the argument that fluid infusion may lead to overload and reduce the persons' comfort' (MacKinlay 2006, p.223).[2]

At all times, the dignity of the person must be upheld. There are a number of interventions that can be of no benefit to people who are dying, and that may cause extra distress. It is then that the palliative approach to care should be instituted.

---

2   Discussing the case of a woman in a persistent vegetative state with dementia, who had a PEG tube inserted, the judge ruled that 'any form of artificial nutrition or hydration is a medical procedure, not part of palliative care, and that it is a procedure to sustain life, not to manage the dying process' (Ashby and Mendelson, 2004, p.442).

Examples of interventions that might be distressing to people who are dying:

- continuing to treat when it has been recognised by medical staff that further treatment cannot reverse the deterioration of the person's condition
- continuing medications with a goal of cure when body systems are shutting down
- inserting a nasogastric tube or PEG tube to a person in terminal stages of dementia, which causes distress to the person without any real benefit
- giving IV (intravenous) therapy when the person's organs are obviously failing and they are in the process of dying.

A person who is dying should have a palliative approach to care that includes:

- adequate pain relief
- the opportunity to address issues of suffering, including spiritual and religious care as appropriate
- good quality skin care
- all measures that promote the dignity and identity of the person in the process of dying
- the understanding that a person who is dying ceases to be thirsty and only requires sufficient fluids to keep their mouth moist.

13

THE FINAL DAYS AND HOURS OF THE JOURNEY

There are still many things that we do not understand about the process of dying and death. Over the years, first as a nurse and then later as a priest, I have been privileged to be a part of this journey on many occasions. Each death is different, and sometimes the end comes quickly; sometimes it takes days, perhaps even longer. Barbato (2002, 2005) suggests that getting an estimate of the time until death may distract people from what is happening, and may lead to greater anxiety. This view is also held by Mal and Dianne McKissock (1995), leading authorities on grief. There is a sense in which some people hold onto life, even as they are dying. I remember well one woman, Joan [not her real name] who was in the final stages of life, no longer able to eat or drink, extremely weak; all her clinical signs showed she was very near to death and yet, it seemed she could not die. Both she and her husband were Christians. Tom [not his real name] continued to believe that God would heal her, and Joan was aware of that. At some point Tom came to realise that Joan's healing would be in her dying; then her suffering would be ended and she would be with God. It seemed that she knew when this happened; perhaps it was the way that he now prayed with her; it is difficult to say, but it was at that point that she died, in peace at last. If we are able, giving the person permission to die is a very wonderful gift. Saying whatever it is that you need to say to the person then is important, even if you think that he or she may not be able to hear, or to understand. Sometimes, that is all that is needed for death to come.

THE MYSTERY OF DEATH AND DYING

Michael Barbato (2002, 2005) has written of the mystery that surrounds the process of dying. Part of this process, for some people, is a lapse into unconsciousness. This may happen for varying periods of time. One of Barbato's patients, Pam, was so deeply unconscious that 'she did not react when a catheter was inserted into her bladder.' Her state remained the same for some days. Imagine his surprise when several days later, phoning to see if the she was still alive, he found:

> She was eating, drinking champagne and entertaining the family. It was her birthday. There was a dramatic deterioration over the next 24 hours but she was still aware and extremely peaceful. Twenty-four hours later she was once again unconscious and died shortly after. (Barbato 2002, p.129)

Sometimes people are aware of conversations held while they were apparently unconscious, as can be attested to if they regain consciousness. Sometimes people who have been unconscious will regain consciousness to say goodbye to loved ones, and then die. Michael Barbato has written more extensively about these phenomena, including near-death experiences, in his book *Caring for the Dying* (Barbato 2002).

Some people will wish to have their family with them as they die, and will wait to have this happen; others will choose to die when the family has just slipped out of the room for a moment. Some people apparently experience deathbed visions. There are many differences, and this should not be surprising, as in life people are also very different in the ways they respond to life. Barbato has summed up this sense of mystery around dying well in the following words:

> Our brain is a wonderful organ but it contains and limits consciousness to such a degree that conscious awareness is confined to worldly things. It finds it difficult to include the mystical and the mysterious, including the concept of immortality. In its 'mind's eye' death is final and tells us our consciousness dies with our physical body. The Dutch philosopher Spinoza believed otherwise, and 430 years ago said that true happiness and contentment is contained in *sub specie aeternitatis* – that is, seeing everything from the perspective of eternity. (Barbato 2002, p.143)

SIGNS THAT DEATH MAY BE NEAR

There are a number of markers that indicate that death is near, the most obvious of which are:

- loss of consciousness
- changes in breathing pattern
- changes in circulation.

When loss of consciousness occurs, continue to speak to the person, touch them and be present to them, pray with them, if that is what they would want. In other words, continue to act normally around them, and above all, do not start talking over them and ignoring their presence. They may comprehend much more than you think.

Changes in breathing often occur in the last days and hours before the time of death. A sign that death is near is the onset of a pattern of breathing with a cycle of deep sighing, then shallow breaths, then breathing stops for a short time. This is called Cheyne-Stokes respiration, and is a clear sign that death is near. Even though this may sometimes sound distressing to those listening – as, for instance, when there is a gurgling sound from secretions in the back of the throat – the fact that the person doesn't cough means that he or she is already unconscious and will not be distressed by this.

Changes in circulation are also common when death is near and the circulation begins to shut down. This will be seen in blueness of lips, fingers and toes, and the skin may take on a mottled appearance.

By the time the person has experienced these changes, he or she will also have stopped eating, and the only thing needed then is to keep the mouth moist. Urinary output will diminish as well – another sign that the body is closing down, and death is near.

During this waiting time, families may wish to be with the person who is dying as much as possible, but different family members may feel differently about this. There is no rule that applies here. But in these dying days, hours and moments, comfort is the main aim of care. This includes maintaining the person on pain relief as needed, even if he or she seems to be unconscious. Restlessness may be a sign of pain in an unconscious patient. Pain may also be experienced as a result of being in the same position for too long, and so gently turning and repositioning the person, and giving gentle back massage, are additional means of touch and intimacy. Keeping the skin comfortable through sponging or bathing in bed is also an important comfort measure and opportunity for touch.

At death, breathing will have stopped and the body will begin to cool and become stiff. It is best to lay the body flat, turn off any electric blanket and room heating, turn off oxygen and phone the doctor or nurse. As Barbato (2002, p.158) helpfully notes, do not call the ambulance and do not phone 000, as these calls may result in CPR being instituted 'unless there is clear documentation to the contrary'. This is not a time for resuscitation; rather, it is time to allow death to occur with a sense of dignity and peace.

AT THE TIME OF DEATH

At the time of death it may be important to mark it in some special way. It is OK to kiss your loved one, to hug them, or speak to them. You might even like to think about what to do, in preparation for this time. For the person who has a religious faith, it is most appropriate to have a representative of that faith come for this time. There may be prayers, reading of Scripture, perhaps the lighting of a candle (see Chapter 7, 'Responding to Meaning: Symbol and Ritual').

14

LEARNING TO LIVE WITHOUT MY PARTNER

THE JOURNEY INTO A NEW LAND

'Learning to live without my partner' is yet another learning experience on this journey. In recent years, we have learnt more about the process of grieving, and most authorities now acknowledge that grief does not end at a set time, and that in fact the relationship continues, albeit in a changed state. A life-long partner is not forgotten after a year – or ever! Even dysfunctional relationships are remembered. But at some point the grieving person will come to the realisation that the partner who has died is not coming back alive.

A TIME TO GRIEVE

How long should I grieve, what is 'normal'? There is no set time. Markers along the journey do help. I am often struck by the ways that different cultures and religious groups mark the passing in death of one of their members. I think that sometimes adherents of the mainline Protestant churches do expect grief to have an ending.

In the story of Wendy that follows you will note that she has been asked by people about finding a new partner, and hear her distress at what she felt was the assumption that she was supposed to be 'over' her grief and moving on in life. Grief does need work, and to move on too quickly to find relationships to replace the loss may not allow the grieving person to really do the work of grieving.

THE JOURNEY WITHOUT A PARTNER

There are a number of tasks to work through in this process, and remember, there is no set time frame within which these will happen:

- finding meaning in life without the presence of the loved one
- keeping the memories alive and relevant
- marking and celebrating the life
- allowing sadness to emerge
- finding new interests
- taking time.

As we have stated earlier, grief does not just happen once a loved one dies. Whether through chronic illness, ageing or cancer, we have been grieving throughout the process of change. Now our loved one is no longer physically with us, our journey of grief continues. As Doug Manning writes:

> Part of the pain in grief is caused by the necessity to move from the present to memories. Part of the healing of grief happens as we learn to draw comfort and warmth from memories. (Manning 1991, p.2)

Some ideas that could prove helpful at this stage include:

- Find a good friend who is willing to talk and listen with you, about the person who has died.

- Write a poem or story or continue with your journal. Some people find it useful to write a letter to the person who has died, saying all the things they wish had been said.

- Go to the places you used to go to with your loved one. Sometimes enjoying this routine will help you reminisce.

- Reflect and/or write a list of blessings that you shared with the person during your lives together.

- Music or other forms of art may be very therapeutic (Wei and Levkoff 2000).

- Compiling a book on something that was special to the person who has died. Anne Hand's father loved to photograph flowers, plants and animals and to write poetry. She said: 'When he died, I gathered many of his photographs and poems and compiled them into a book and gave this to my mother to help her, and me, keep this aspect of my father alive.'

Wendy continued to reflect and write after her husband's death.

It is now nearly 22 months since Lewis died and more recently I have been reflecting on where I am with my life journey. I have continued to accept all invitations (even if I wasn't that keen) and have kept myself busy with playing music, volunteer work and my church. There is still what I call the hiccups of grief when people show too much compassion. There are also the odd times when missing my Lewis so much that the tears flow.

On the first anniversary of Lewis's death I had just completed three months of volunteer work in a Christian village in West Bali. I felt so very much loved in Blimbingsari and know that many were praying for me back in Australia. So that day as I was leaving I heard this wailing sound. It was the children from the village school weeping because I was leaving. I really didn't have much time to reflect on what had happened a year ago and a group from my church had just joined me the night before. The timing was not planned but I know God had input. The whole time I was in the village I felt the presence of Lewis and with God's help achieved what I would have never been able to do under my own strength.

People ask me how I am. The usual answer is 'I'm fine'. Having been brought up not to complain and knowing people don't really want to know if you are not fine, for whatever reason, this keeps others happy. Spiritually my faith is growing and I know I have moved into a stronger relationship with God. However, I continue to have this emptiness within me. I go through the motions of coping well and really don't have financial or health problems. I can still express compassion and have no doubt that my strong maternal protection of my family continues, but I lack the ability to respond emotionally to major changes and situations, even with the family. I go through the appropriate motions but I don't feel comfortable about this. And no, I am not depressed; God's love continues to surround me. When I put Lewis's ashes under a dwarf eucalypt tree recently I thought it would be an emotional time, but no. I knew that Lewis was with God and this was just his earthly remains.

Sometimes I feel I am marking time before I join Lewis. For me this may arise out of having such a close relationship with Lewis and one I felt secure in. We did everything together and were open in all we did and felt. I have noticed that I am now more direct in voicing my opinions or concerns. But I have many times seen that in elderly people and I do feel that it is an honest approach. The one problem with this is that others hope I will do the talking for them.

Although I planned to live alone there has always been someone staying for long periods. Currently a granddaughter studying at the Australian National University has been with me for 11 months. God's plan? I will stay in this large house until I can no longer cope.

It has been unhelpful when it is suggested I will find another partner. For me this is not an option and shows that grief is often not understood, nor its duration. I know some see me as having coped well with Lewis's death, which I have, but they see it as now in the past.

I have tried explaining to Christian friends my current feelings of emotional emptiness but they quickly change the subject. Even after Lewis died I had no spiritual guidance from my priest. Not through lack of care, but I feel from not knowing how to respond. For many mentioning death is uncomfortable. Lewis and I never talked about death; he wanted to pretend it wasn't happening. Remember, no one told Lewis his death was fairly imminent, including the doctors. One palliative nurse gave me a pamphlet dealing with death, and that was not our regular nurse. Another friend, a priest, asked Lewis if he was worried about what his future held – that was the closest anyone came to.

Looking back I realise that there were another seven deaths of family and friends who died in the few months after Lewis's death. Including one elderly Christian lady I had been visiting for over 20 years, an aunty and a childhood neighbour. Maybe I am holding back with my feelings from others as this might protect me from grief if they die, or sadness if situations change.

During the winter of 2010 I will return to Blimbingsari for two months. My journey without Lewis continues with God's love. I feel secure in that, and I know He will help me with this inner emptiness. I am reminded of the TIS[1] 687 song, first verse:

> *God gives us a future, daring us to go into dreams and dangers on a path unknown.*
> *We will face tomorrow in the Spirit's power, we will let God change us,*
> *for new life starts now.*

(Wendy Elliott, May 2010)

THE JOURNEY CONTINUES

Life is punctuated by loss and the accompanying grief, yet there are positive aspects to grief and loss. Part of this is to come to a realisation that we can and do grow and mature through our grief and loss. Hopefully there is also the realisation that we are not alone in this process of dying and death; there are people to whom we can turn for help and support, if, at times, only to listen to us.

This book has been an attempt to deal with some of the more challenging matter around this important topic. It is hoped that these words, in part or in full, have been helpful to you, as a reader.

---

1   *Together in Song* (TIS) hymn book.

LEADING CHRONIC DISEASES OF OLDER PEOPLE

LEADING CHRONIC DISEASES OF OLDER PEOPLE IN AUSTRALIA[1]

1. **Dementia:** It is estimated that in 2008, 6.8% of the population aged 65 and older had dementia (p.173).

2. **Heart disease:** It is estimated that in 2007–2008, 3.4 million Australians of all ages (16.5% of the population) 'had one or more long-term diseases of the circulatory system' (p.142).

3. **Chronic lung disease:** It is estimated that in 2010 2.3% of the Australian population (of all ages) has emphysema or bronchitis (p.177).

4. **Diabetes:** An estimated 4.0% of the population in 2007–2008 'had been told by a doctor or nurse that they had diabetes (excluding those with gestational diabetes)' (p.154). For community-dwelling (not residing in aged care facilities) males aged 65+, approximately 16% had type 2 diabetes, and for community-dwelling females 65+, approximately 11% had type 2 diabetes (p.322).

---

1   All bracketed page references in Appendix I relate to: Australian Institute of Health and Welfare (2010) *Australia's Health 2010.* Canberra: Australian Institute of Health and Welfare.

LEADING CHRONIC DISEASES OF OLDER PEOPLE IN THE UK[2]

1. **Cardiovascular disease:** Main components are ischaemic heart disease (IHD), also called coronary heart disease (CHD). Prevalence increases with age.

2. **Arthritis:** The most common is osteoarthritis, which affects 60% men and 70% women over the age of 65 years.

3. **Diabetes:** Virtually all cases in people over the age of 65 years are cases of type 2 diabetes, especially prevalent in those who are obese.

4. **Chronic lung disease and asthma:** Chronic lung disease is one of the largest causes of death worldwide. Asthma can be difficult to distinguish from chronic lung disease in older people, results in a reduced quality of life.

---

2   Health Survey for England 2005, Volume 2. Chronic diseases: The Health of Older People. Available at www.ic.nhs.uk/webfiles/publications/hseolder/vol2.pdf.

LEADING CAUSES OF DEATH OF OLDER PEOPLE

LEADING CAUSES OF DEATH OF OLDER PEOPLE IN AUSTRALIA[1]

1. The leading *underlying broad causes of death* for older people in Australia vary by age.

    ○ For Australians aged 65–84, the top four broad underlying causes of death are as follows:

      * cancer and other tumours (37.5% for males, 33.3% for females)

      * cardiovascular disease (31.6% for males, 32.4% for females)

      * respiratory system diseases (9.5% for males, 8.8% for females)

      * endocrine-related disorders (4.1% for males, 4.8% for females).

    ○ For Australians aged 85+, the top four broad underlying causes of death are as follows:

---

1   All bracketed page references in Appendix II relate to: Australian Institute of Health and Welfare (2010) *Australia's Health 2010*. Canberra: Australian Institute of Health and Welfare.

* cardiovascular disease (42.3% for males, 48.6% for females)

* cancer and other tumours (20.2% for males, 12.1% for females)

* respiratory system diseases (11.6% for males, 8.7% for females)

* mental disorders (5.9% for males, 8.3% for females) [dementia is included as a subsection of mental disorders] (p.51).

2. The leading *specific causes of death* for older Australians (65+) are as follows (figures are for 2007):

    ° The two leading causes of death for both males (26%) and females (29%) were coronary heart disease and cerebro-vascular diseases, with stroke being the most important of these.

    ° The third most common cause of death for females (8.5%) and sixth most common cause of death for older males (4.5%) was the category of dementia and Alzheimer's disease.

    ° Cancer was also common, with lung cancer being the third most common cause of death for older males while fourth for females. Colorectal cancer, prostatic and breast cancers were also common causes of death.

    ° Lung diseases, notably chronic obstructive pulmonary disease, including emphysema and diabetes were also common causes of death (pp.325–326).

LEADING CAUSES OF DEATH OF OLDER PEOPLE IN THE UK

1. The leading *underlying causes of death* for older people in the UK aged 75 years and over are (figures are for 2006–2008):

   - cardiovascular disease – 34.5% (34% for males, 34.9% females)

   - cancer – 21.6% (26.2% for males, 18.4% for females)

   - respiratory disease – 16.4% (16.7% for males, 16.1% for females)

   - 'other' causes – 27.5% (23% for males, 30.7% for females).

   'Other' causes include: dementia, neurodegenerative diseases, external causes (accidents, suicides, homicides), gastrointestinal conditions, diseases of the genitourinary tract and others.

2. As for Australia, the underlying causes of death vary according to age:

   - 75–79 years – leading underlying cause of death is cancer (33.4%)

   - 80–84 years – leading underlying cause of death is cardiovascular disease (34.3%)

   - 85–89 years – leading underlying cause of death is cardiovascular disease (36.8%)

   - 90 years and over – leading underlying cause of death is cardiovascular disease (35%).

3. The ten most common underlying causes of death in people aged 75 and over are:

   - chronic ischaemic heart disease – 10%

   - pneumonia, organism unspecified – 7.4%

- ° acute myocardial infarction – 6.2%

- ° stroke, not specified as haemorrhage or infarction – 6.0%

- ° other chronic obstructive pulmonary disease – 4.7%

- ° malignant neoplasm of bronchus and lung – 4.2%

- ° unspecified dementia – 4.1%

- ° other cerebrovascular diseases – 2.9%

- ° senility – 2.8%

- ° heart failure – 2.2%.

REFERENCES

Adamle, K.N. and Ludwick, R. (2005) 'Humor in hospice care: Who, where and how much?' *American Journal of Hospice and Palliative Medicine 22*, 4, 287–290.

Ahmad, S. and O'Mahony, M.S. (2005) 'Where older people die: a retrospective population-based study.' *QJM* 98, 12, 865–870.

Albom, M. (1997) *Tuesdays with Morrie.* New York: Doubleday.

Alzheimer's Australia (2005) *What is dementia?* Available at www.alzheimers.org.au/common/files/NAT/20100804-Nat-Helpsheet_1.1-What_is_dementia.pdf, accessed on 12 September 2011.

Ashby, M.A. and Mendelson, D. (2004) 'Gardner re BWV: Victorian Supreme Court makes landmark Australian ruling on tube feeding.' *Medical Journal of Australia 181*, 8, 442–450.

Australian Government/NHMRC (2006) *Guidelines for a Palliative Approach in Residential Aged Care.* Canberra: Australian Government Publishing.

Barbarto, M. (2002) *Caring for the Dying.* Sydney: McGraw Hill Book Company.

Barbato, M. (2005) 'Caring for the dying patient.' *Internal Medicine Journal 35*, 10, 636–637.

Best, M. (2010) 'The ethical dilemmas of euthanasia.' *CASE 25*, 4–9.

Birren, J.E. and Cochran, K.N. (2001) *Telling the Stories of Life through Guided Autobiography Groups.* Baltimore, MD: The John Hopkins University Press.

Bourgeois, S. and Johnson, A. (2004) 'Preparing for dying: Meaningful practices in palliative care.' *Omega 49*, 2, 99–107.

Brennan, F.P. and Dash, M. (2009) *Stories from Palliative Care.* (Desktop-published.)

Brennan, F. (2010) 'Ethical challenges in palliative care.' *CASE 25*, 18–21 and 27.

Bryden, C. and MacKinlay, E. (2002) 'Dementia: A Spiritual Journey towards the Divine: A Personal View of Dementia.' In E. MacKinlay (ed.) *Mental Health and Spirituality in Later Life*. New York: Haworth Press.

Carroll, L.P. and Dyckman, K.M. (1986) *Chaos or Creation: Spirituality in Mid-life*. New York: Paulist Press.

Cayton, H., Graham, N. and Warner, J. (2004) *Dementia: Alzheimer's and Other Dementias at Your Fingertips* (2nd edition). London: Class Publishing.

Connor, J. (1997) *A Funny Thing Happened on the Way to the Nursing Home*. New South Wales: Bookbound Publishing.

Cousins, N. (1981) *Anatomy of an Illness as Perceived by the Patient*. New York: Bantam Books.

Dean, R.A.K. and Major, J.E. (2008) 'From critical care to comfort care: sustaining the value of humour.' *Journal of Clinical Nursing 17*, 8, 1180–1095.

Deck and Folta (1989) in B. De Vries (2001) 'Grief: intimacy's reflection.' *Generations XXV*, 2, 75–80.

De Vries, B. (2001) 'Grief: intimacy's reflection.' *Generations XXV*, 2, 75–80.

Dunne, K. (2004) 'Grief and its manifestations.' *Nursing Standard 18*, 45, 45–51.

Ellershaw, J. and Ward, C. (2003) 'Care of the dying patient: the last hours or days of life.' *British Medical Journal 326*, 7379, 30–34.

Festa, M.N. and Tuck, I. (2000) 'A review of forgiveness literature with implications for Nursing Practice.' *Journal of Holistic Nursing Practice 14*, 4, 77–86.

Frankl, V.E. (1984) *Man's Search for Meaning*. New York: Washington Square Press.

Gibson, F. (2004) *The Past in the Present: Using Reminiscence in Health and Social Care*. Baltimore: Health Professions Press.

Goldsmith, M. (1996) *Hearing the Voice of People with Dementia: Opportunities and Obstacles*. London: Jessica Kingsley Publishers.

Goldsmith, M. (2001) 'When Words are No Longer Necessary: The Gift of Ritual.' In E. MacKinlay, J. W. Ellor, and S. Pickard (eds) *Aging, Spirituality and Pastoral Care: A Multi-national Perspective*. New York: Haworth.

Gott, M., Small, N., Barnes, S., Payne, S. and Seamark, D. (2008) 'Older people's views of a good death in heart failure: Implications for palliative care provision.' *Social Science and Medicine 67*, 7, 1113–1121.

Gregory, J.E. and Gregory, R.J. (2004) 'The spirit feather: An ecologically based celebration of life.' *Journal of Palliative Medicine 7*, 2, 297–300.

Heinz, D. (1994) 'Finishing the story: Aging, spirituality and the work of culture.' *Journal of Religious Gerontology 9*, 1, 3–19.

Hide, K. (2002) 'Symbol, Ritual and Dementia.' In E. MacKinlay (ed.) *Mental Health and Spirituality in Later Life.* New York: Haworth.

Hudson, R. and O'Connor, M. (2007) *Care of the Dying: A Practical Approach to Aged Care.* Melbourne: Ausmed Publications.

Hughes, J.C., Louw, S.J. and Sabat, S.R. (eds) (2006) *Dementia, Mind, Meaning, and the Person.* Oxford: Oxford University Press.

Kastenbaum, R. (2000) 'Death Attitudes and Aging in the Twenty-First Century.' In A. Tomer (ed.) *Death Attitudes and the Older Adult: Theories, Concepts, and Applications.* Philadelphia, PA: Brunner-Routledge.

Kenyon, G.M., Clark, P. and de Vries, B. (eds) (2001) *Narrative Gerontology: Theory, Research, and Practice.* New York: Springer.

Kestenbaum, I. (2001) 'The gift of Healing Relationships: A Theology of Jewish Pastoral Care'. In D.A. Friedman (ed.) *Jewish Pastoral Care.* Woodstock, VT: Jewish Lights.

Killick, J. (2004) 'Dementia, Identity and Spirituality.' In E. MacKinlay (ed.) *Spirituality of Later Life: On Humor and Despair.* New York: Haworth Press.

Killick, J. and Allan, K. (2001) *Communication and the Care of People with Dementia.* Buckingham: Open University Press.

Kimble, M.A. (2003) 'Final Time: Coming to the End.' In M.A. Kimble and S.H. McFaddon (eds) *Aging, Spirituality and Religion – A Handbook.* Vol 2. Minneapolis, MN: Fortress Press.

Kitwood, T. (1997) *Dementia Reconsidered.* Buckingham: Open University Press.

Koenig, H.G. (1994) *Aging and God: Spiritual Pathways to Mental Health in Midlife and Later Years.* New York: The Haworth Pastoral Press.

Kubler-Ross, E. (1970) *On Death and Dying.* New York: Collier Books/ Macmillan Publishing Co.

Lewis, M.M. (2001) 'Spirituality, counseling, and elderly: An introduction to the spiritual life review.' *Journal of Adult Development 8*, 4, 231–240.

Linton, A.D. and Lach, H.W. (2007) *Matteson and McConnall's Gerontological Nursing: Concepts and Practice* (3rd edition). St Louis, MO: Saunders Elsevier.

Lo, B., Kates, L.W., Ruston, D., Arnold, R.M. *et al.* (2003) 'Responding to requests regarding prayer and religious ceremonies by patients near the end of life and their families.' *Journal of Palliative Medicine 6*, 3, 409–415.

Lugton, J. (2003) *Communicating with Dying People and Their Relatives.* Melbourne: Ausmed Publications.

MacKinlay, E. (2001) *The Spiritual Dimension of Ageing.* London: Jessica Kingsley Publishers.

MacKinlay, E.B. (2006) *Spiritual Growth and Care in the Fourth Age of Life.* London: Jessica Kingsley Publishers.

MacKinlay, E. (2008) 'New and Old Challenges of Ageing: Disabilities, Spirituality and Pastoral Responses.' In E.B. MacKinlay (ed.) *Ageing, Disability and Spirituality: Addressing the Challenge of Disability in Later Life.* London: Jessica Kingsley Publishers.

MacKinlay, E. (ed.) (2010) *Ageing and Spirituality Across Faiths and Cultures.* London: Jessica Kingsley Publishers.

MacKinlay, E., McDonald, T., Niven, A., Russell, F. and Seidel-Hooke, D. (2010) *Final report: Minimising the impact of depression and dementia for elders in residential care.* Canberra: Centre for Ageing Pastoral Studies. Unpublished report.

Mako, C., Galek, K. and Poppito, S.R. (2006) 'Spiritual pain among patients with advanced cancer in palliative care.' *Journal of Palliative Medicine 9*, 5, 1106–1113.

Manning, D. (1991) *Permission to Grieve. Continuing Care Series, Book 4.* Texas, TX: In-Sight Books.

McFadden, S. and Hanusa, M. (1998) 'Nourishing the spirit in long term care: Perspectives of residents and nursing assistants on sources of meaning in residents' lives.' *Journal of Religion, Spirituality and Aging 10*, 4, 9–26.

McKissock, M. and McKissock, D. (1995) *Coping with Grief* (3rd edition). Sydney: ABC.

Metzger, D. (1993) 'Writing for your Life.' In R.I. Morgan (ed.) (2002) *Remembering Your Story: Creating Your Own Spiritual Autobiography.* Nashville: Upper Room Books.

Mickley, J.R. and Cowles, K. (2001) 'Ameliorating the tension: Use of forgiveness for healing.' *MICKLEY 28*, 1, 31–37.

Mitchell, G., Murray, J. and Hynson, J. (2008) 'Understanding the Whole Person: Life-Limiting Illness Across the Life Cycle.' In G. Mitchell (ed.) *Palliative Care: A Patient-centred Approach.* Oxford: Radcliffe Publishing.

Morgan, R.L. (2002) *Remembering your Faith Story: Creating Your Own Spiritual Autobiography.* Nashville, TN: Upper Room.

Netto, N.R., Goh, Y.N.J. and Yap, L.K.P. (2009) 'Growing and gaining through caring for a loved one with dementia.' *Dementia 8,* 2, 245.

Niven, A. (2008) 'Pastoral Rituals, Ageing and New Paths into Meaning.' In E.B. MacKinlay (ed.) *Ageing, Disability and Spirituality: Addressing the Challenge of Disability in Later Life.* London: Jessica Kingsley Publishers.

Nouwen, H.J.M. (1994) *Our Greatest Gift: A Meditation on Dying and Caring.* London: Hodder & Stoughton.

Pargament, K. (1997) *The Psychology of Religion and Coping: Theory, Research, Practice.* New York: Guilford Press.

Pierce, G. (2006) 'Loss, grief and family carers of older people.' *Grief Matters 9,* 1, 15–18.

Phillips, L.R. and Reed, P.G. (2010) 'End-of-life caregivers' perspectives on their role: Generative caregiving.' *The Gerontologist 50,* 2, 204–214.

Reid, M. (1996) *The Journey to Emmaus: A Way to Care for People Facing Death.* Melbourne: The Joint Board of Christian Education.

Running, A., Girard, D. and Woodward Tolle, L. (2008) 'When there is nothing left to do, there is everything left to do.' *American Journal of Hospice and Palliative Medicine 24,* 6, 451–454.

Sacks, O. (1998) *The Man Who Mistook his Wife for a Hat and Other Clinical Tales.* New York: Touchstone. ('The Lost Mariner', pp.23–42.)

Shuman, J. (2003) 'The Last Gift: The Elderly, the Church, and the Gift of a Good Death.' In S. Hauerwas, C.B. Stoneking, K.G. Meador and D. Cloutier (eds) *Growing Old in Christ.* Grand Rapids, MI: William B. Eerdmans.

Steinhauser, K.E., Clipp, E.C., McNeilly, M., Christakis, N.A., McIntyre, L.M. and Tulsky, J.A. (2000) 'In search of a good death: Observations of patients, families, and providers.' *Annals of Internal Medicine 132,* 10, 825–832.

Stevens, J., McFarlane, J. and Stirling, K. (2000) 'Ageing and Dying.' In A. Kellehear (ed.) *Death and Dying in Australia.* Melbourne: Oxford University Press.

Tolson, C.L. and Koenig, H.G. (2003) *The Healing Power of Prayer.* Grand Rapids, MI: Baker Books.

Thompson-Richards, J. (2006) 'Joy in the Midst of Suffering: Clowning as Care of the Spirit in Palliative Care.' In E. MacKinlay (ed.) *Aging, Spirituality and Palliative Care.* New York: Haworth.

Wei, J. and Levkoff, S. (2000) *Aging Well: The Complete Guide to Physical and Emotional Health.* New York: John Wiley & Sons, Inc.

Wilkes, L. (1998) 'Reflection on the Good Death and the Nurse in Palliative Care.' In J. Parker and S. Aranda (eds) *Palliative Care: Explorations and Challenges.* Sydney: MacLennan & Petty.

Wolterstorff, N. (1987) *Lament for a Son.* Grand Rapids: William Eerdmans Publishing Co.

World Health Organization (2010) *WHO definition of palliative care.* Available at www.who.int/cancer/palliative/definition/en, accessed on 12 September 2011.

INDEX